T0161888

NEVER A DULL MOMENT

→ NEVER A DULL MOMENT

Honest Questions by Teen Agers

with Honest Answers

by

Eugenia Price ◁————————

Turner Publishing Company
Nashville, Tennessee
www.turnerpublishing.com

Copyright © 1955, 2020 Eugenia Price

Never A Dull Moment

No part of this publication may be reproduced, stored in a retrieval system, or transmitted in any form or by any means, electronic, mechanical, photocopying, recording, scanning, or otherwise, except as permitted under Sections 107 or 108 of the 1976 United States Copyright Act, without either the prior written permission of the Publisher, or authorization through payment of the appropriate per-copy fee to the Copyright Clearance Center, 222 Rosewood Drive, Danvers, MA 01923, (978) 750-8400, fax (978) 750-4744. Requests to the Publisher for permission should be addressed to Turner Publishing Company, 4507 Charlotte Avenue, Suite 100, Nashville, Tennessee, (615) 255-2665, fax (615) 255-5081, E-mail: submissions@turnerpublishing.com.

Limit of Liability/Disclaimer of Warranty: While the publisher and the author have used their best efforts in preparing this book, they make no representations or warranties with respect to the accuracy or completeness of the contents of this book and specifically disclaim any implied warranties of merchantability or fitness for a particular purpose. No warranty may be created or extended by sales representatives or written sales materials. The advice and strategies contained herein may not be suitable for your situation. You should consult with a professional where appropriate. Neither the publisher nor the author shall be liable for any loss of profit or any other commercial damages, including but not limited to special, incidental, consequential, or other damages.

Cover design: Bruce Gore

Library of Congress Cataloging-in-Publication Data Upon Request

9781684426492   paperback
9781684426508   hardback
9781684426515   ebook

17 18 19 20 10 9 8 7 6 5 4 3 2 1

To My Dad

CONTENTS

Except where otherwise noted, Scripture quotations contained herein are taken from the Berkeley Version of the New Testament, translation by Gerrit Verkuyl. *Copyright 1945 by Gerrit Verkuyl. Published by Zondervan Publishing House.*

The author and publishers wish to thank the Moody Bible Institute and the Moody Press for permission to quote from The New Testament, A Private Translation in the Language of the People, by Charles B. Williams. *Copyright assigned to the Moody Bible Institute, 1949. Published by the Moody Press.*

PREFACE

This book is written primarily for young people. The questions came to me directly from high school and college students, and without these questions (which went sailing straight to the point in almost every case!) I could never have "pulled the book together" at all! More than that, I was certainly stimulated and made to face some issues which up to the time of the writing of this book, I had simply tried to side-step!

From the age of twelve to about fifteen or sixteen, I had these same questions. I did *not* get the answers that satisfied me. As a result, at seventeen I considered myself an atheist! I realize this is extreme. Few people go that far. But all of us need to have the claims of God upon our lives untangled for us. All of us need to have the deep things of God simplified. All of us need to be shown and reminded that God did just this Himself, when He came to earth to live in the Person of Jesus Christ. He *simplified* things!

All of us need to know that it is not a matter of our preference whether or not we agree with Jesus Christ. God has already decided this for us. After all, He is God. We are not. But those of us who have tried it know that He decided it all the *right* way. The *only* way that works. And it is a Way of freedom and good times!

Did you get that?

I have found from my own experience, after having tried *both* God's Way and my own, that *His* is not only the one that *works*, it is much more fun than mine ever was!

This *is* a book for young people.

But there may be many occasions when some teenager will give it to Mom or Dad for a birthday present. Why? Because it is for those who are not only young in years, but *young in the Christian life as well.* And over and over again I learn of some really *alive* Christian teenager who has dared to live Jesus Christ in front of his or her parents until one happy day the parents too tumble into the Arms of the same waiting Lord! And so, this is a book for all persons "new" in the Kingdom of God!

My very best thanks go to Dr. Robert Cooke, President, Youth for Christ International; Dr. Harold Warren, North Baptist Church, Flint, Michigan; the Rev. Mr. Richard Halverson, Hollywood Presbyterian Church, Hollywood, California; Mr. Jim Rayburn, Director of the Young Life Campaign; Mrs. Billy Graham; Miss Angelyn Dantuma, Dean of Women, Moody Bible Institute, Chicago, Illinois; Mr. Dan Ankerberg, Hi-C Club Director, Chicago, Illinois; Dr. Paul S. Rees, First Covenant Church, Minneapolis, Minnesota; Rev. Mr. Lund, Redeemer Lutheran Church, Milwaukee, Wisconsin; Dr. Remo I. Robb, National Youth Director, Reformed Presbyterian Church; Mrs. Fannie Davis, I. A. H. Foundation, Elgin, Illinois; Miss Rosalind Rinker, Inter-Varsity Christian Fellowship, Seattle, Washington; Miss Evelyn Rounds, First Baptist Church, Eau Claire, Wisconsin; Mrs. Stan

PREFACE

Keldsen, mother of a teen-ager; Miss Sherry Lee Smith, a Christian teen-ager; Mrs. Virginia Matson; and my friend Ellen Riley, faithful associate who was a mixed-up teen-ager *with me* many years ago . . . for their excellent comments and help on the book in manuscript form. To the same Mrs. Stan Keldsen and Miss Lillian Mangels for their expert typing and corrections, and to Miss Betty Carlson for her splendid cooperation in distributing manuscript copies to be read . . . more of my very best thanks. And last, but far from least, to all the young people in colleges, high schools, junior high schools, church young people's groups, and summer camps . . . probably the shiniest THANKS of all for those right-to-the-point questions you gave me!

To Ruth Settles, Director of MYF at the South Park Methodist Church in Canton, Illinois, so much *more* than "thanks" for the patience and love and real Calvary caring given me from the very beginning of the preparation of this book.

And to the One who not only gave me the answers but who *is* the *Answer* . . . "Thank You, Lord, from the depths of a grateful heart, and please make Yourself as *real* to everyone who reads this book as You have become to Genie Price, who could never have written it if You hadn't reached down and *picked her up* out of her own deep, dark confusion!"

I have tried what is in this book. From experience I know it works. I have tried to write it so it would not be over my own head! So, I know it won't be over yours! I love every single one of you or I would never have *dared tackle* a book like this!

One more thing . . . the title is true too. I've found the Christian life to be anything but dull! But if you still think it is dull, here's an offer: read all the way through this book, then live in a *close walk* with Jesus Christ for one year and if you find you're really *bored* in the Presence of God, write me a letter and I'll write the book all over again!

EUGENIA PRICE

Chicago, Illinois

1

Why Bother About God?

"Why get so serious about God? (I'll be old soon enough!)"

This is a lulu of a question!

I picked it for a starter because it takes us straight to the point in a hurry and unless there is an answer that makes sense, I might just as well not try to finish the book.

But there *is* an answer.

And it *does* makes sense! Think with me now.

We know we can stake the safety of our daily lives *on* the absolute fact of the law of gravity. We can build on it. It is a *fixed* thing. It is so absolute and so unchangeable that we'd feel like idiots if we said: "Why get so serious about the law of gravity?"

Anyone who lies awake at night because he or she is afraid the bed is going to float up through the ceiling because the pull toward the center of the earth might go out of commission, had better have his or her head examined!

In a hurry.

The law of gravity works because the "pull" is directed toward the center of the earth and does not vary!

We want to be sure the houses we build don't sail off their foundations and so we build them being dead sure and quite serious about the law of gravity.

We "get so serious about gravity" because we want what we build to stay on the ground!

You have asked me a question: "Why get so serious about God?"

I don't blame you at all for asking it. And I believe I can give you an answer which will interest you because I lived from your age to the ripe old age of thirty-three *not* taking God seriously at all!

Now, before we say anymore, let's really find out what you meant when you used that word "serious" in the question you asked. It would seem to me that you meant something distinctly unpleasant and dull. We associate the word "serious" with sour-puss expressions and faces all drawn up from trying to be religious and "do what's right." I imagine that when you think of "taking something seriously" you'd like to run.

If you remember, the end of the question said: "I'll be old soon enough!" And that tells me that around in your mind, when you asked that question, prowled the tired, old idea that "taking God seriously" means—no fun!

"Aw, religion's for little kids and old ladies with lace collars!"

I remember saying that over and over from the age of thirteen to about sixteen, when I decided to forget about God altogether.

So, you see, I *do* know exactly what you mean, when you ask, "Why get so serious about God?" And add, "I'll be old soon enough!" And if you think of the word "serious" as dull and unpleasant, forget it. That isn't the way I use it at all. I might have used it that way once. But not anymore.

When we take something "seriously" I simply mean we are *not* ignoring it! We are reckoning with it as being real. How far would you get by *not* taking the law of gravity seriously when you lean out a twelfth-story window?

That law is *absolute!* The fact that *you* choose not to take it *seriously* does not change the fact that gravity *is*. And when you lean too far out that twelfth-story window, you may ignore it, but you are *not* going to break the law of gravity or prove that it doesn't matter—*you* are going to *illustrate* it!

"Why get so serious about God?" Because God *is* and we simply cannot walk around Him or ignore Him or change Him or forget Him *if* He has revealed Himself to us as He really *is* — in the Person of Jesus Christ!

It is easy to take any other religion or leave it. Other religions do not claim what Christianity claims. Jesus Christ stood right up and declared: "I am the Way and the Truth and the Life; no one comes to the Father except through Me" (John 14:6).

That is a big statement!

Jesus Christ stands right in front of us and says things which we simply cannot ignore *if* we are intelligent, wide-awake people who want to think for ourselves!

Jesus looks at you and says: "Follow Me."

Now.

He doesn't say, "Follow Me anytime after fifty-five years of age!" He says, "Follow Me—now."

Jesus Christ says, "He who is not with Me is against Me, and he who does not gather with Me, scatters" (Luke 11:23). That is to say, whoever is not in partnership with Jesus Christ is against Him.

He does not hedge! There is never a third way with Jesus Christ. That's one of the reasons why we *can* worship Him. He is absolute! He says *this* or *that* and nothing else will do. We can respect and worship a God like that. He is not woolly and sentimental and wishy-washy. We can depend upon Him.

He Is God!

And for that reason He dares to say what He says.

Whether we want to reckon with Jesus Christ or not, He is here, looking at us, confronting us with Himself saying: "Follow Me." And He alone can *be absolute*. The deities in the other religions appear to be content just to sit on some distant throne and flap a bored eyelid at us poor struggling creatures down here. But in the Gospel of Jesus Christ, God, Himself, arranged a visit to this old earth in the Person of Jesus, the Son of Man, and lived out under human conditions the kind of life He wants us to live! And not only did Jesus live here under these sometimes difficult human conditions, He went the whole way!

He died on the Cross and He rose again from the dead!

For us.

These two facts are absolute! We can stake our eternal lives as well as our daily lives on them. The *facts* that Jesus died on the Cross and rose from the dead are *fixed facts*. You may doubt them. I did for years. But they were still true even while I laughed and showed my stupidity by refusing to believe them.

Sometimes you may say to me, "But, I don't understand what the death of Christ on the Cross has to do with me." Maybe you don't yet. We won't ever understand all of it in this life. But if you are one of those, who, like myself, have "gotten way off the beam" in your life, you know what it means to feel your heart *ache* for forgiveness.

Jesus died on that rough, splintery Cross because He wanted to do away with that "thing" in us that made us "get off the beam." That "thing" is in even the most well-behaved people. And a good close look at your disposition might show up your need for Jesus, even if you have never committed any of the so-called big, "sinful" sins.

And even if His Death doesn't seem to have much to do with you now, the very fact that you are reading this book and have read this far, *proves* that you *do* believe He rose *from* the dead! You at least suspect that Jesus Christ is alive, or you wouldn't be reading!

Right now, let me ask you one thing: What would your reaction be if God decided not to take *you* seriously until you're much older? He couldn't ignore you without now and then forgetting your oxygen supply, you know. That would be just one way things would change.

You don't need to answer this question now.

Just think about it.

Would you mind if God forgot about you for a few years?

2

What's Right and What's Wrong?

"How do I know what's right and what's wrong?"

"How do I really know what's wrong, when so many people tell us something different?"

"What if I don't like to do the things that are right! What then?"

I am using all three of these questions because they each seem to show up different sides of the big issue— What "goes" and what doesn't "go" in the life of a Christian?

First of all, let me tell you right now that it is over *this* question that many people stumble *away* from God in their teens! I know this is true from my own teens. I fully understand *anyone* who declares that Jesus Christ is someone with a big, black beard who is out to spoil the fun in life! I thought that too, once. So, I went as far the other way as I could go. I became an atheist!

(If you are fighting God, remember, I fought Him too until I found out what He is really like!)

You can take my word for it, God is not a divine "wet blanket." Jesus Christ doesn't frown at us and shout, "No!", expecting us to jump through a "celestial hoop" just because He wants us to be "nice." He tells us to do what He tells us because nothing else really works!

He was right there in the beginning when we were created. If Jesus Christ is God's revelation of Himself, then He and God are One. God was there at creation. So was Christ. They are really closer than Father and Son, but that's about all our minds can understand. Jesus Christ is not only the Saviour, He is the Creator God, too. And if we think that the mechanic knows more about how a complicated machine runs than the man who invented it, we had better think again.

The inventor knows best how his invention works. He knows what makes it run smoothly, produce the most goods, and what kind of care will make it last the longest.

Just as the inventor knows best about his machine, so the Creator knows best about His creation. God knows what will make things tick for us. We don't! We didn't create ourselves, did we? If we were self-created beings, then, of course, we would know what would give us the most benefit and pleasure and make us more productive in the long run. If we had created ourselves, we *could* ignore God. We wouldn't have needed Him in the first place.

But God created us.

God thought us up!

God created that energy that seems ready to burst out of you every minute! God created those muscles that crave activity. God created the muscles in your face that enable you to laugh! He created the sense of rhythm that makes you respond to music. He created boys so that at a certain age they would like to look at girls. And He also created girls so that they would like to look at boys. He created the need for sleep and the need for food. Hunger is God's idea. He planned it that way.

Whoever has the idea that all the things God wants you to do are dull, must not like to swim or listen to music or eat or have dates.

Jesus went around when He was here on earth, saying, "Be of good cheer." That may sound meaningless to us, but remember that Jesus spoke in the language of His earthly day. And in the language of our day, He would have walked into a group of teens and said, with what must have been the most wonderful smile in the world, "Hello, kids. Have fun! Use up that energy; I gave it to you to use!"

Now, no doubt you are saying, "But, what if I don't like to do the things Jesus calls 'right'? What if being a goodie-goodie doesn't spell fun for me? What then?"

What then?

This. We are not going to talk about "right things or wrong things." Instead, I'm going to ask *you* a question: Do you think Jesus Christ could be phoney? Do you think He could be what you might call a piker-God? Would He stand up and say, "Follow Me," if He knew that we were going to be miserable following Him? Would

He have said, "I have come so they may have life and have it abundantly"—if He meant to spoil everything? Either Jesus Christ lied when He said: "I have talked these matters over with you so that . . . your joy be made complete," or He simply did not know what would bring us joy—enjoyment, fun.

But if he created us, shouldn't He know what we'd really enjoy most?

Yes, of course He should.

And he said: "Be of good cheer"—have fun. But He also said: "Follow Me." And that means following Him according to His teachings, all of which are just *too hard* for us to follow *if* we try to follow them in our own strength, with the wild, unruly, selfish natures with which we are all born!

Now you may be asking, "What goes on?"

God seems to be saying, "Do this," even in the face of our inability to do, or our actual *dislike* of the thing He tells us to do.

Is God really that hard?

Does God expect the impossible of us?

Yes, God expects us to be a way which in our own natures we cannot be.

God expects us to do things we don't like to do.

God expects us to love everyone and think of other people *always* before we think of ourselves. God expects us to love our enemies. He expects us to do something nice for everything nasty someone else does to us!

God expects too much!

Yes, He certainly does.

What's Right and What's Wrong?

But . . . He expects too much of *us*, not of Himself. And if now, right at this point, you can lay hold of this great bit of information, you will understand all the rest of what we have to say. Your mind will begin to turn with some thoughts of its own. You will begin to see "dawn breaking." You will begin to think: "Yeah, I catch on to this whole thing now! I've been going at it all backwards!"

This will be true with you *if* you will allow Christ to open your mind and your heart and your very life to *this* great, breath-taking, exciting, adventure-packed offer of God's!

God expects far more than we can do under our own steam, out of our own unruly, off-beat natures—*BUT,* He doesn't intend any of His teachings for our own *human* natures! At conversion, when we turn to Christ, we say we "receive" Jesus Christ . . . small children say, "Jesus comes into my heart." And they're exactly right! At that tremendous, life-changing moment we do just that. We change lives! We give God our old wayward, wild, unruly, selfish lives (or natures) and then God puts His Own Life — a BRAND NEW LIFE right *into* us. And since God and Jesus and the Holy Spirit are One (the Trinity) that means that through the Holy Spirit, who comes right inside us to live when we receive Jesus Christ, *God Himself* comes in!

The Holy Spirit can sound awfully far away and vague.

When we mention the Holy Spirit a lot of people yawn. *But,* the reason most people are bored with religion and church is that they do not know that God

Himself, in the form of the Holy Spirit, can literally penetrate our bodies and live His Own Life *in us!*

Does it sound impossible?

It is from a human point of view.

But with God all things are possible, and this is *God* with whom we're concerned.

Did you get that? Maybe you should read it again, or maybe we can just say it another way: When you opened the door of your life to God, by asking Jesus Christ to come in and dwell within you, you were *not* just repeating words! HE CAME IN!

And if you are *willing*, and give Him the full "go ahead," He will begin to work within you to change you so that you will not only *want* to do the things which Christ wants you to do; you will gradually get to *prefer* them. God will *change* your desires.

The same Power that brought Jesus up out of that grave is released *in us* when God comes to indwell us!

That "life-giving power" is actually a spiritual law in the same way the law of gravity is a physical law. It is a sure thing.

It can't fail.

God backs it up with His Own Life.

Does it sound dull to you that you can be changed so that you will *prefer* to do what Jesus Christ asks of you?

Look up at the sky on a clear night and try to imagine what human being could think up something one millionth as exciting as those systems of planets and moons and constellations of stars swinging and wheeling up through all that endless, endless space!

Even if man could think them up—could he control them?

Before you decide definitely that God's way is dull, or before you live through one more day just half-in and half-out of the Kingdom of God — remember that night sky and remember that God is nothing trite and dull and commonplace whom we can take or leave.

And your life will begin to move toward that big, momentous time of receiving God's Own Life entirely into yours, the very *minute* you begin to realize fully that we're concerned with God because God is so terribly concerned with us!

Doesn't it *do* something to you when it hits you that the God who hung those stars out there and actually thought up atomic power is constantly concerned about the person who goes by your name and who lives at your address?

3

Is Sincerity Enough?

"If one is sincere about what he believes, is he right?"

No.

Sincerity *is* a fine trait to possess.

But, it is not enough.

Even sincerity in our prayer-time is not enough.

We will go into the subject of prayer later on, but if we are asking God for something which is *outside* His Will for us, no matter how sincere we are in asking, He cannot answer. God knows what we *really* need and He would not be much of a God if He allowed our sincerity to sway Him when He knows the thing for which we ask would do us harm in the long run.

No, sincerity is not enough.

We can be sincere and be dead wrong!

Is Sincerity Enough?

I remember the look on a woman's face once when she told me the only guide she needed was her conscience. "If my conscience hurts, then I know a thing is wrong."

I remember the look on her face because I replied, "My dear friend, then you must have the only conscience of its kind in the world!" I was a young Christian and probably that was a smart-alecky answer. What I meant was this: We can trust our consciences *only* when they are Christ-controlled consciences. Why is this? Simply because when they are not Christ-controlled they are *self-controlled!* For eighteen years I had my conscience so trained that it bothered me not at all toward the end of my old life! At the age of thirty-three, just before my conversion, my conscience was hardened. No doubt it started out tender and sensitive as with most children. Some of us more than others feel real pain when we hurt someone or when we disobey our parents. My friend, Ellen, who helped me arrive at some of these answers, and who led me along my stumbling road to Christ a few years ago, tells a story about herself when she was an overly sensitive child with a conscience that was painfully alive! Ellen and I are old enough so that when we were very small, some houses were still lighted by gas jets which had to be ignited with a match. One night, being afraid of the dark, she asked her mother to light the jet in her room about three times. When her mother thought Ellen had fallen asleep, she would turn out the gas. Then Ellen would wake up and want the light again!

Finally, after the third time, when her Mother stood beside her with the half-burned match in her hand, little

Ellen began to cry. All of a sudden she didn't care about the light anymore! Her conscience was stabbing her like a big sharp pin because she had caused her Mother so much trouble!

That is one extreme. My hardened thirty-three-year-old conscience was another. We may begin with a tender conscience and end with none at all or one so well controlled that it is no longer a guide to anything but our own selfish ends.

For example, circumstances train our consciences when we are not even aware of it. Constant disobedience hardens them. If you steal something once and get away with it and then do it again, the third time you do it, your conscience may do no more than pinch a little. Is that a guide you can trust?

"I am sincere and do the best I can," sums up the "religion" of many thousands—many millions of well-meaning people on the face of this old earth. But it is *not* enough.

Here is an illustration which punches home what I mean. As long as a river stays within its banks, it *gets* somewhere. It flows, and factories can use its water power, providing it is a big enough river. Even if it is a small river, as long as it stays within its banks, it causes no floods and it holds pleasure for fishermen and life for the fish fortunate enough to dodge the fishermen.

But—when the river overflows its banks, it becomes a *swamp!*

Do you get the point?

Unless we have some guideposts—unless we stay

within banks—we become swampy! We have no power. We cause heartache and we flood our own lives and the lives of those around us with the backwater of our stupid and sometimes sinful actions.

We have already established that we all need a *fixed-point* upon which we can depend. We need a starting place. That Place is Jesus Christ. And when we are rooted and grounded in Him and are obeying Him, our lives will flow right along with power and purpose. We'll *get* somewhere. The Bible sets forth the Way of Christ. We can think of the Bible as our "river banks." Or as our road-map. And the Bible tells us that we are all born with the kind of out-of-gear nature that *needs* to be changed, redeemed, traded for a new one before we can trust even its sincerest intentions to be right!

It is so easy to be *sincerely* mistaken and pursue a course that is in direct opposition to God's Will for us.

There is no place where it is easier to be "sincerely mistaken" than in the realm of romance! We may *sincerely* want to be with someone, but we may be completely mistaken in our "sincere" notion that he or she is good for us!

At these points we come face to face with the *big* Question with a capital "Q"! Do I love myself more than I love Jesus Christ? Or do I love Jesus Christ more than I love myself?

Of course, if you are not a Christian, you love yourself best. Unfortunately many Christians also love themselves best. And it is quite possible to be a Christian of sorts and still not have a Christ-controlled conscience and heart! It is quite possible and not at all unusual for a Christian believer to be "sincerely mistaken." And surely he cannot chart his course on his own sincerity in this case.

Sincerity does not make us right.

Only the Holy Spirit of God living right in us day in and day out makes us right. And in the eyes of God, we are never forgiven simply because we are sincere, but we are *always* forgiven when we state our cases to God on the grounds of what Jesus Christ did for us. It is not our sincerity (important as it is); it is our belief in what Jesus did on the Cross for us. God does not forgive us and make us new because *we* are sincere. He forgives us because our faith in Jesus is sincere. This does not belittle us. It raises us to the highest place. Cooperators with God! Sons of God! And it is the only way God can bring us into close companionship with Himself. You see, God is holy. Sin is anything that keeps us away from God! So sin is just the opposite of being holy. God wants us to be one with Him. Jesus prayed that we would be one with Him the night before His enemies crucified Him! He wanted it so much that He shed His own Blood so that we would *see* and believe that we were created to be friends with God. And when Jesus died, a Power was released on the Cross that wipes out our sin when we put our faith in the One who hung there!

If this fact doesn't mean much to you now, accept it and begin to follow Jesus; and *as you walk with Him* through the years, He will reveal it to you as you are able to understand it.

Is Sincerity Enough?

God the Father was not angry with us. He did not force Jesus to die because He was a bloodthirsty God! The Bible tells us very plainly that "God was *in* Christ" right there on that Cross "reconciling the world [us] to Himself!" We were so far out of line that God knew *nothing* short of showing us what the inside of His Great Heart really looked like could change us! And to see inside a heart, we must see blood! On the Cross, God let His Own Heart break in that tremendous moment when He *took* our sinful natures into His Own Heart and smothered them to death! It broke His Heart, but it also breaks the power of sin in our lives — *when* we make an eternal agreement through Christ with the God who loved us enough to die for us! Enough to take *our* sin into His Own Heart. Enough to take our place on the Cross and let us go free.

When something is big and dangerous, drastic action is needed to wipe it out.

God took that drastic action on the Cross.

The desire in us all to look after our own interests first (which is the basis of all sin) was so big and so dangerous that God had to take drastic action!

Jesus said, "No one has greater love than this: to lay down his life for his friends." He gave His life because He loved us so much He wanted us to be *free* from the law of sin and death!

All this is *so much more* than just "being sincere."

This is being Christian. And being truly a Christian means among many other things that we have a clean slate with God because of what Jesus did, *when* we receive Jesus as our Personal Saviour and go on to follow Him as our Lord and Master.

Being Christian is being truly alive now and forevermore.

"For God so loved the world that He gave His only begotten Son, so that whosoever believes in Him should not perish, but have everlasting life" (John 3:16).

God, in His Holy Word did not say, "For God loved the world so much that anyone who is *sincere* may never perish but have eternal life." He said, ". . . whosoever believes in Him [Jesus]."

Sincerity *cannot* cancel sin.

Sin is a drastic thing. Look in your mind's eye at Jesus hanging on the Cross. Realize that He was God, and then ask yourself how serious God thinks sin is! As you "look" at God Himself hanging on a Cross to break the power of sin in our lives, can you honestly think *sincerity* could be enough?

4

Do I Have to Go to Church?

"Church is so boring!"
"Church is no fun!"
"I go to Sunday school. I've worshiped the Lord there, haven't I? Why do I have to stay for church?"
"If I do everything else God wants me to do, can't I get out of going to church?"

Of all the people on the face of this bumpy old earth who should *not* be bored or boring — it's Christians! So, let me ask a few questions!

Is your church a Christian church?

Does a Christian church mean that it is a church belonging to Jesus Christ?

Did Jesus say: "Where two or three have gathered in My name, I am there with them"? If your answers are "Yes" that means He is there at Sunday morning church service as well as with your intimate group of close friends which meets for prayer in your home or at school.

"Where two or three have gathered in My name, I am there with them"! (Matthew 18:20)

So, Jesus Christ is right there in church with you on Sunday morning. Jesus Christ and God are one and the same, so the God who thought up microscopic atoms and put a fury of power in each one, is there too.

And you're bored?

Now, before you have a chance to say: "Yeah, but God doesn't preach the sermon or sing the solos!" or, "Yeah, but I can't see Him!" . . . let me say this: primarily we don't go to church to be entertained. If we do, then our motives are wrong. If you go to a football game to have your mind developed, or if you eat a big turkey dinner so that you might have a good piano lesson next week, something's out of gear!

The point in going to church is to worship God.

And even if you have never really listened all the way through a sermon, why not try it once? Might surprise you. Or, try *not* looking at your watch or the clock on the wall through just *one service* and "look" with your mind's eye at the face of Jesus Christ instead. Sit there and think who He is! What He did for you. Picture Him literally raising Himself up off that cold slab, in that dark, blood-encrusted tomb the first Easter morning and walking slowly out into the bright sunlight of His own Resurrection Day! He must have walked slowly at first— and maybe He blinked His Eyes and rubbed them because He had been dead! And that Resurrection Light is bright!

It *has* to be bright.

Do I Have to Go to Church?

It *is Resurrection* Light. Brighter than any light we can imagine because it is the Light created by the Power that flowed through the dead and broken Body of the Lord Jesus and brought Life back into Him!

We gasp at atomic and hydrogen power!

Neither can bring life, can it?

The power that God poured into the dead body of Christ that first Easter morning makes atomic energy look pale and weak!

That was the Power and Energy of God.

That is the same Power and Energy that flows through us when we receive Christ as our Personal Saviour and invite Him in the Person of the Energizing Holy Spirit to come and dwell within us!

That Power flows through your body as you sit there in church — *if* you are a Christian.

And you're bored?

If the fellow or girl you love is in the room where you're sitting—are you bored?

Do you love Jesus Christ? Or does He bore you?

If He bores you, then you need not be ashamed. Simply get to know Him as He really is. Because knowing Jesus Christ Personally makes you immune to boredom!

Try sitting there in church next time, really focused on the Person of Jesus Christ and see what happens!

"I go to Sunday school. I've worshiped the Lord there, haven't I? Why do I have to stay for church?"

That's the next question on the subject of church. And here again, it will be a very good idea to examine your motives for asking a question like that. Or better still, try to figure out why it is you even went to Sunday school!

It sounds to me very much as though you go because you think you have to. Or because you *do* have to, according to Mother or Father or Aunt Minnie!

And I suppose it is better to go that way than not to go, but you are not only missing the *point* of going, you are missing the *meaning* of going. If it means obeying a law or a rule someone else sets down for you, then you have not caught the wonder and excitement of New Testament Christianity!

Is Christianity something to get excited about?

The disciples who *knew* Jesus was the Son of God thought so! Remember in the Gospel of Luke, when they shouted and sang and made so much noise, as Jesus was riding into Jerusalem, that the Pharisees (men who loved religion better than they loved God!) asked Jesus to make His friends calm down?

And do you also remember what Jesus said to the Pharisees who had nothing to laugh about and so couldn't see why the disciples felt so gay and happy? This is what Jesus said:

"I tell you, if these keep silence, the stones [here along the road] would (at once) cry out"! (Luke 19:40).

There was so much Glory and Gladness in the air that day because Jesus *was there* that He knew perfectly well it had to burst forth somewhere! If the disciples fell silent and looked bored and moped along as though following Jesus were a duty, then *something had* to "sound off!" The Joy was there because Jesus was there! No use trying to stop the disciples from shouting at the top of their lungs. They were happy. Jesus was there with them! He was their Master. They were His disciples. That meant Joy.

What about *you* on Sunday morning?

If you're His disciple and He's your Master, you're going to show it in some other way more attractive to behold than a long face!

Are you His disciple?

"If anyone wants to come after Me, he must deny himself, take up his cross day by day and follow Me" (Luke 9:23).

Do you qualify?

Are you willing to say "no" to yourself when you know you should?

Are you willing to "take up [your] cross day by day," that is, are you willing to assume the responsibilities which are rightly yours? And are you following Jesus Christ continually?

If you qualify, if this is true of you, then you are His disciple.

Just as surely as was John or James or Peter as they walked along beside Him along those dusty roads of Galilee almost two thousand years ago.

That's your part in finding joy in church. You must really *be* a disciple of Jesus Christ.

But just *being* a disciple is not enough. That isn't the reason the disciples made so much noise that day. They shouted for joy because *Jesus was there* and they knew he was King!

What about you in church?

Is Jesus there with you?

He's there or He told us a lie.

Remember what He said?

"Where two or three have gathered in My name, I am there"!

Was Jesus telling the truth when He said that?

Are you His disciple?

Are you still bored with the idea of church in the light of all this?

"If I do everything else God wants me to do, can't I get out of going to church?"

I rather imagine you could answer this last one yourself. Again, we have that old matter of motives. This question sounds like one opponent trying to trap another! Is God your enemy? Or is He Love?

If God is Love, why do we want to "get out" of being with Him?

And if He isn't Love, then the Bible is lying!

This question of yours sounds as though you are trying to strike a bargain with God, doesn't it?

"Oh, Lord, I will read the Bible for Thee providing Thou wilt let me out of going to church on Sunday!"

That's pretty silly, because in the first place, we don't read the Bible so that *God* can get to know *us*. We read it so that *we* can get to know *God!* God already knows us. We read it so that we can learn. Not so that God can learn. He already knows everything.

God made a New Covenant with us when Jesus Christ came. Remember? There is no Law now that says "do this and do that" in so many words. The *power* of the truly Christian life is that four-letter word which everybody in the wide, wide world loves — LOVE!

If you don't love God, then you don't *know* Him.

I don't blame you for getting furious when someone forces you to go to church if you don't know God at all. Because if you don't know Him, of course you don't love Him. It would be just a duty then. And no one really likes doing things for duty's sake!

But doing things for love's sake is a totally different thing!

Turn this over in your mind. If you love someone you want the world to know, and you seem to love all the other people who love your beloved! Isn't that right?

Doesn't it stand to reason that if we love Jesus Christ, we want the world to know? We *like* to make "public appearances" with Him. That's the way it is on Sunday morning and on Sunday evening.

We like to be where our Beloved is.

He's with us always, that's for sure. But at church we openly let other people know we love Him and belong to Him. And that's a good feeling instead of a bore, *when* we really love Him. We also like to be with other people who feel about Him the way we feel.

If some of the people who go to your church seem not to love Him, maybe you need to help them get more of an idea of what He's really like! Could this be true? You see, when we begin to think in terms of what we can do for the One we *love*, it all becomes something else entirely.

And the "dull moments" are all crossed out!

5

Can a Christian Be Popular?

"I'm afraid of being different! Can I be popular and still be a Christian?"

"Can a Christian be popular?"

"I don't like to be different! I want to be a part of the gang." Is that what troubles you? I can understand that very well. It's natural. But remember? We're talking about the *SUPER*natural! On a purely human level, *before* God's Spirit has come to live right *in* you, it's too hard to be thought different. You can't take it. Neither could I. But *after* you are converted, *after* you have received God's Life into yours, the entire picture *can* change.

The gang at school of which you're afraid won't necessarily change (at least not at first), but *YOU* will, *if* you want to!

Can a Christian Be Popular?

Before we go any further into this point, let's look at some words of Jesus Himself—*about* Himself. (Remember, if we can't believe Jesus Christ, whom *can* we believe?)

Jesus said of Himself: ". . . I, when I am lifted up from the earth, shall draw everyone to Myself" (John 12:32). It's true Jesus was telling His disciples what kind of death He would die (lifted up on a cross), but I believe there is a deeper meaning in these words, and this meaning has a direct bearing on our practical, down-to-earth everyday lives! Jesus said: "I, when I am lifted up . . . shall draw . . ." That means that if Jesus is lifted up, He will *attract* people to Himself. I can tell you that is absolutely true, because that is the way I became a Christian. Ellen Riley, the girl who was my close friend in my teens, and who eighteen years later led me to Jesus Christ, simply let me *see* Jesus Christ living His Life through *her* life! I could see that she had something I didn't have. And I wanted it. She "lifted up" Jesus Christ and He *drew me* to Himself through her. Jesus Christ living in her had "lighted up" her personality with His Personality.

I had lived in the world for a long time. I had "been around," as we say. I had worked to acquire what the world calls sophistication. I spent more money than was necessary on my clothes; I lived at an address that kept me broke paying the high rent, because I thought it added to my possibility of being a success—of "being popular." But here was Ellen, *glowing* with something I couldn't quite define or even label!

She didn't do any of the things I thought I had to do in order to "have fun." I offered her a cigarette (the day we met again, after not having seen each other for eighteen years) and she smiled at me and said very politely, "No thank you, I don't need them now." I offered her a drink. The same thing happened. A very pleasant smile and a polite "No thank you, I don't need it now."

Was she different?

She certainly was! Did I make fun of her? I certainly did. But the upshot of the whole thing was that after awhile I, who thought I knew all the answers about finding pleasure and being "popular" and well liked, found that what *she* had was so attractive I couldn't resist trying it too!

Within six weeks I was an excited new follower of Jesus Christ!

And I am more excited about Him now at the end of six *years*.

What am I driving at?

Just this. Attractive people are *going* to be well liked. The big reason Christians are not popular (when they're not) is that they are *not* attractive!

This is most unnecessary, because Jesus Christ *is* attractive when we see Him as He *really* is. When He actually *lives within* us, we should be the most attractive people in the world!

Now, by "attractive" I don't necessarily mean that all Christian girls will be cover-girls and all Christian boys will be handsome, romantic heroes! I mean "attractive" in the sense that they will *draw* other people to them because of an inner magnetism, a love for other people, an inner poise and a keen, clean sense of humor—all so "tops" that they could come only from God Himself, and therefore can only be possessed by Christians who, in turn, are possessed by Christ!

There is no charm school in the world where a young woman can find the secret of a smile that comes because there is *no fear* behind it! And if perfect love casts out fear, the Christian should not be afraid. And if we are not afraid, then right there an enormous pile of complexes and social stumbling blocks are eliminated!

The Christian young lady can learn to enter any room full of people with poise and grace. Why? Because she can enter on the Arm of Jesus Christ!

The Christian young man can learn to meet new people well because the same Lord Who showed such power and poise when the old Pharisees tried to confuse Him, actually meets those new people through Him.

Does this sound fine in theory but not workable?

Are you thinking, "Yeah, but she's in her late thirties—that might work after people are old and tired. Young people are sometimes nervous and not very sure of themselves and non-Christians can get pretty nasty!"

Admitting freely to thirty-nine years (but refusing to admit that *any* Christian needs ever to be "old and tired"), I agree that we all get nervous and unsure and that any non-Christian can be cruel. But these claims I make for the attractiveness of the Christian life are for the *truly* Christian life!

They do not hold true for the boy or girl, man or

woman, who has merely been "saved." They do not hold true necessarily only if our doctrine is "correct."

They hold true *ONLY* if we have allowed the Holy Spirit to so change us *all the way* to the depths of our beings that *we,* and our old jittery, nervous *un*attractive personality traits don't blot out the Poise and Charm and Gentleness and Strength and Love of Jesus Christ Himself!

In other words we can get hold of a few facts *about* Jesus Christ, tuck a Bible under our arms, put a handful of tracts in our pockets and go about trying to "do people good" and end up doing the glorious cause of Jesus Christ more harm than we can possibly imagine. You see, non-Christians are not as impressed with what you *believe* as they are impressed with what you *are!*

Dwight L. Moody once said that Christians are the world's "Bible." The world won't read the Bible, but it *will* watch the behaviour of Christians! And so what we *are* is so much more important than what we *say.* After all, if there are certain activities enjoyed by your friends who are non-Christians or lukewarm Christians, and you feel you cannot take part in those activities, don't act superior about it. Don't look down your nose at them and feel holier-than-thou! Don't go about shunning them or making pious remarks about *your* salvation and *their* sin. Don't make remarks about them at all.

LOVE THEM.

More about this business of loving those who do not see eye to eye with you in the next chapter.

For now, we are concerned with *your* popularity

as a Christian among non-Christians. And I say that not only is it possible for a Christian to be popular, he or she really should be *extremely* popular!

I know you're thinking about your *small* Christian group at school, or perhaps you're absolutely alone in following Christ . . . in the midst of the hundreds who do not follow Him. But after your non-believing classmates watch you go through a few years of finals with a confidence and inner poise and peace they never heard of at exam time, they'll begin to envy you. And you can have this confidence and this poise and this peace *if* you have allowed the Holy Spirit to do as He pleases in you. If you keep your path to God clear.

They will want your courage in the face of danger, your good judgment, your strength to go on when tragedy strikes your life. None of these traits will "hold up" in the tight places *everytime*, except for the Christian. The Christian believer has access to them all. Not all at once, because we must all learn how to *take* God's gifts. But even in the new Christian, that "something" which is of God breaks through to attract and to draw.

I do not mean to give the idea for one minute that you as a Christian young person will not come in for your share of hard-knocks. You will be misunderstood over and over again. But one of the deep secrets of the victorious Christian life is that we must *be willing* to be misunderstood!

Jesus understands what we're doing with our lives. People — even other Christians — may not always understand. We must accept that, draw on the sense of humor readily available for *all* believers in Jesus Christ, and just — go on.

Jesus not only understands *us;* He understands the people who make fun of us. He warned us about it, in fact, in so many words! "Blessed are you when they slander and persecute you . . . because of Me" (Matthew 5:11). And He goes on to say your reward will be great in heaven, so "be glad and supremely joyful" (Matthew 5:12).

Moreover, the truly victorious Christian does not *bear* or merely grit his teeth and *endure,* he or she actually grabs hold of hardship in the Name of Christ and makes good *use* of it!

How? By showing those who persecute and abuse you that you are safely *out* of the realm of self-defense. That something that would make another "blow his top" doesn't phase you because you are *alive!* You see, being *alive* makes all the difference.

People say, "How can you waste your life by just being good? You only live once! How can you throw that life away on Christ?" That's where we have the last laugh, if we have put our faith in Jesus Christ. Because *we are never going to die.*

The *essential part* of us—that which makes us "ourselves" and not someone else—*lives on eternally, consciously,* in the very Presence of Jesus Christ, in the company of other selves.

The Christian who has caught the holy "hilarity" of God knows that popularity sought for itself does not last. Frankly, it's the greatest freedom in the world to be

Can a Christian Be Popular?

free of the mob! When you are free of minding what people think of you, then and only then are you free to *love* those people! Because as long as you are letting them shape your life and dominate your thinking, you are too apt to be afraid of them or suspicious of them and therefore unable to love them.

I know several Christian girls who have won popularity contests in high school and college. I honestly believe there would be more Christians winning popularity contests if more Christians would be willing to let Jesus Christ take over *every area* of their lives.

After all, the few things a Christian teen cannot do (unless he or she wants to hurt Jesus Christ) would fill a *very few* of the hours in a week. If you are truly Christian and let the Love and Joy and Peace and Gentleness and Kindness and Good Humor of Jesus Christ come through you in the classroom, in the corridor by your locker at noon, in the gym, on the athletic field, in the social clubs, *you'll be popular!* No one likes a selfish uncouth, sarcastic, impolite bully—even if he *is* a football hero! No one likes a flippant, overdressed, bored, gossipy female—even if she is "from the best family" and smitten with her own looks!

Did you ever hear anyone describe a true follower of Jesus Christ as being selfish, uncouth, sarcastic, impolite, flippant, overdressed, bored and gossipy? Real Christians show the *opposite* of all these ugly personality traits!

Can a Christian be *popular?*

What do *you* think?

6

How Can I Love Everybody?

"How can I love kids who do things I don't do or even approve?"

Is there just a touch of "look at me, I'm better than you" attitude in this question? Wouldn't you say offhand that this person needs another look at the stories about Jesus Christ when He was here living on this earth? Didn't Jesus eat and talk with sinners? What about the Samaritan woman at the well? Jesus broke a hard and fast rule of society by asking her for a drink of water. No Jew ever held social conversation with a Samaritan! But Jesus did. And she was *converted* as a result of His making an effort to reach her *where she was* in life—not by looking down His nose at her because she wasn't *where He was* in morality and doctrine!

Also, the question is phrased by one who, at least

subconsciously, claims a right to "approve" or "disapprove" the actions of others! Jesus told us *not* to judge. We are only responsible for *Our Own Behavior,* so responsible for it that it must be of the high, clean, attractive variety that will show the behavior of others to be what it is *WITHOUT* our having to point the condemning finger!

I would say that the Christian who wrote this question has apparently missed the point of *love* altogether. To him or to her, "love" is evidently regulated by the *conduct* of other people!

Suppose Jesus had loved us *only* when we were behaving according to His high standards of holiness! Where would we be now?

If you are a Christian believer, do you follow me? Can you see the spot in which this question falls apart? Isn't it on the word "love"?

Let's look awhile at *LOVE* itself. Jesus tells us to love our neighbor. And loving one's neighbor does not mean simply that we are to love the people who live next door, or the people who *agree* with us.

Loving our neighbor means that we are to love everybody!

Everybody?

Yes, everybody.

But what about the people who rub us the wrong way? What about the unattractive people who don't like the things we like? How can a Christian *love* a roughneck would-be hoodlum who already has his name on the police blotter at sixteen? How can a Christian boy *love* the braggart whose favorite topic of conversation in the locker-room is how many bottles of beer he stowed away last Saturday night?

Well, assuming you are a Christian, *now* is the time to remember this: If the kids you know at school are *not* Christians, you cannot expect them to love and obey God. Nor can you expect them to love you unless you are extremely lovable to them! I do not mean that you will need to take part in some of the things which they do. I mean that you *must* love them and *not* feel superior to them. And you *can* love them because "the love of *God has been* shed abroad in your heart" by the Holy Spirit Who lives within you. Your part is to let that love come out! If your parents are not Christian believers, if the Holy Spirit has never been invited into their lives, then do *not* expect them to behave like Christians. Your part is to show them the love of Christ until they want what you have!

So, we do not need to expect the non-Christian necessarily to love his neighbor. But what about the Christian? Yes. Jesus says *we must love everyone.* But how can we? Well, what does love really mean? Unfortunately we have sung so many popular songs about "moon and June" where love is concerned, most of us think that in order to love someone we must be, in some way at least, *attracted* to that person. This is not what real love means at all! Love, of the kind the Lord Jesus intends that we shall have for our neighbor, means "concern." It means that we are as *concerned* about the welfare and happiness of our neighbor as we are about our own! We cannot be "attracted" to everyone, but we can know a genuine *concern* for everyone, PROVIDING God lives within us. Providing we are Christians in the truest sense and are *willing* to love everyone. If we are willing, then God will love them *through* us!

Now, during the years in which I have been a Christian I have discovered that Jesus Christ never asks anything that is unnecessary. We may not understand His reason, but the Lord Jesus can see the *whole picture* around us. I don't believe anyone could doubt that *love* makes everyone feel better. If you have just been kissed by your mother and told that she loves you, it's a lot better than having been scolded or ignored, isn't it? Anyone knows that. And so this thing called love is well worth going after! God is right.

We agree love is great and that Jesus told us to love. But how? If you are told not to participate in the same forms of entertainment in which certain of your schoolmates take part, not only do you have a right to ask *how* can I love them when they do, but *why* does Jesus say that I must?

He doesn't *say* why!

Jesus Christ seldom explains things. He *changes* us so that we no longer *need* explanations. But don't think I'm dodging the answer to "Why love everybody?" And don't think the Lord Jesus dodged the issue either!

Far from it.

He answers that question along with all the others by the Wonder-filled Thing that He *did* on the Cross. But we have a tendency as Christians to be annoyed or to get angry or dogmatic with those who do not believe as we believe! I know Christian young people who snub or criticize or even make fun of other young people who do not believe or even know that Jesus Christ died on the Cross. They actually act superior to the non-Christian! But Jesus did not demand that we embrace a certain set of rules or beliefs. He said, "Follow Me," and then He went to the Cross and died for us! He said very little. But He *did* it all. He doesn't "tell us off." He *shows* us about Love with His Own Life and His Death and His Resurrection. When we see the true meaning of Jesus' Death for us we only want to be servants to those who don't know Him. I once used to feel that it was right for me to love everyone because each one was a man or a woman or a young person for whom Christ died. *I see something far deeper than that now.* I see that I *must* love everyone not only because Christ loved *them* enough to die for *them* but because this same Christ loved *me* enough to die for *me!* He took the shame of the Cross for me, how can I feel *superior* to anyone?

Is it possible to love everyone?

Yes, it is. But we can all love *everyone* if and *only if* we receive Christ as our Saviour and then follow Him as our Lord. The Christian who will not give Christ His way, cannot love everyone. But he or she *can* surrender completely to the Lord Jesus, just as the non-believer *can become* a believer . . . and as this glorious exciting process goes on and on from one person to another, LOVE *can* rule us all!

Can anyone imagine being afraid of—Love?

Can anyone imagine dodging—Love?

Can anyone imagine thinking LOVE is—*dull?*

7

How Can I Ever Like to Read the Bible?

"How can I get so I like to read the Bible, instead of doing it just because I have to?"

Here again, we are hit with the old complaint—anything to do with God must be dull because it's all tangled up with *duty!* And who likes to do things because someone tells him to do them? "Mother says I should read my Bible. My Sunday-school teacher says I should read my Bible. The minister says I should read my Bible. My Dad says I should read my Bible."

"But I don't *like* to read it!"

"The Bible is dull to me."

"I don't get what it's driving at."

I was thirty-three years old before the Bible interested *me* at all, except for the fact that parts of it I considered to be beautifully written.

In fact, I was almost a year old as a Christian before I really began to get excited about the Bible!

Am I really excited about it now?

Yes.

Do you think I'm crazy for saying a thing like that? You may decide that I can say a thing like that for one of two reasons: I'm off my trolley—or thirty-nine!

And I know that's old.

But I'm *on* my trolley for the very first time in my life!

My life has a *direction* now. I know where I'm going. I'm not trying to fight my way out of a closed paper sack anymore! And one of the ways in which I have become more and more convinced that the Christian life is *THE* life, is through daily reading of God's Own Word—which shows me step by step that my life is *at last* based on Reality. And I can depend on Reality. It's solid.

My Bible tells me that my sins will be forgiven when I put my faith in the Person of Jesus Christ. My Bible tells me that because it is *true.* That's the reason *that* fact is in the Bible—because it is true! Life proves it when we try it. When I put my faith in the Person of Jesus Christ and asked His forgiveness for my sins, it worked. He forgave me!

Now, I did not say that Jesus can forgive our sins *BECAUSE* the Bible says He can. What I said was, the Bible says Jesus Christ can forgive sins because that is a true statement!

Do you the get the difference?

I'm not trying to tell you that things are true simply

because they appear in the pages of the Holy Bible! *My point is that things are in the Bible because they're true!*
Things are not true simply because they're in the Bible.

Things are in the Bible because they're true!

The Bible is God's written-down revelation of Himself. The Bible is made up of many separate books, written by way of many human authors, but a deep study of this amazing library of books within a Book will show that they all tie together and point toward one great Truth: *God's revelation of Himself in the Person of Jesus Christ.*

With a good Bible teacher to guide you, you can read through the pages of the Old Testament and see God trying to reach the hearts of the ancient Israelites with the message of His life-changing Love. You can literally feel the *forward movement* as God's Plan for mankind unfolds. You can sense the ache in the Heart of God, who only wanted to help and save His people, every time you see those selfish, headstrong, sinful people turning their backs on Him, which they did over and over again. The ancient people of God left Him and came back, left Him and came back, left Him and came back. And each time He tried to show them that obeying Him would be easy *if* they would only love Him!

God is still telling us the same thing!

But the difference now is that God stopped trying to show the people by signs and arranged a visit to the earth Himself, in the Person of Jesus of Nazareth the Saviour Who would save His people from their sins. The prophets of the Old Testament, inspired by the Holy

Spirit of God, foretold the coming of the Saviour, and He came. The four Gospels in the New Testament are biographies of the life of Jesus, each with a different theme. But the important thing to us now is that the entire Bible, Old Testament and New, is *ABOUT* Jesus Christ! As we said, the Bible is God's written-down revelation of Himself, and He revealed Himself in the Lord Jesus.

Now, I'm sure there are some who are reading this book right now who will say (or at least think): "So what?"

"Is the fact that the main theme of the Bible is the Lord Jesus Christ enough to make me *like* to read it?"

Yes, it is.

"Not me!"

Yes, you. *IF* you are game enough to open your mind and try something. Do you remember we said that things are in the Bible because they're true? This is not a rash statement of my own. People have been following the teaching of the Bible for centuries and have proven this fact by their victorious lives. So, if you will go along with the fact that things are in the Bible because they're true in the first place, you will have to include this fact too:

"Early the first day of the week, when it was still dark, Mary Magdalene came to the sepulchre and noticed the stone removed from the tomb. Then she ran and went to Simon Peter and to the other disciple whom Jesus loved, and told them, 'They have taken the Lord out of the tomb and we do not know where they have laid Him.' Then

Peter and the other disciple came out and made their way to the sepulchre. The two came running together; but the other disciple ran ahead, faster than Peter and arrived at the tomb first. As he stooped, he saw the linen clothes lying; however, he did not go in. Then Simon Peter came behind him, entered the tomb and saw the linens lying, also the handkerchief that had been around His head, not lying with the linens but wrapped by itself in its particular place. Then the other disciple, who had reached the sepulchre first, entered in too, and saw and believed—for as yet they did not understand the Scripture that He must rise from the dead." Now, this exciting story is quoted word for word from the Gospel of John, from the beginning of Chapter 20 through verse 9 in the Berkeley Version of the New Testament. In the same chapter, a little further on (verse 19) you can read these words:

"As it was evening that same first day of the week and, out of fear for the Jews, the doors were shut where the disciples met, Jesus came and stood in their midst and said to them, 'Peace to you!' Upon saying this He showed them His hands and side, so the disciples were glad to see the Lord."

It would be interesting to you to read the rest of that amazing resurrection story for yourself, because after all it is the only time in the history of mankind that a dead Man was enabled to get up and walk out of a tomb under his *own* power! To me it is almost the most thrilling story there is. (The *most* thrilling is the story of God being willing to become a Baby that first Christmas in order that we might find out for sure what His Nature is really like!)

But if things are in the Bible because they're true, then what I have just quoted to you from the Gospel which John wrote holds the answer to *WHY* you can really learn to *LIKE* to read the Bible!

"Because it has thrilling stories in it?"

No.

"Then why?"

Because Jesus Christ is alive!

He got up out of that tomb and walked out into the world again and then a few days later, after spending some time in last-minute instructions to His disciples whom He loved so much, He ascended into heaven to sit at the right Hand of God the Father. And in the Bible also we read that Jesus Christ is there right now, making intercession (that is, praying for us!). Praying just as He prayed the night Judas betrayed Him (this is in Chapter 17 of the Gospel of John) that we (you and I) should be so close to Him that we should all be just like one! Jesus Christ is alive in His Resurrected Body in heaven where He is One with the Father and He is also *now* able to be right *within* us who belong to Him here on this old earth! We can't begin to understand how Three Persons can be One and how One can be Three, but God is so great that we need these Three Personalities even to begin to describe Him.

If you don't understand about the Trinity, don't let it worry you. No one really *understands* about it. We need only to realize that God showed us in the Person of Jesus what He wanted us to know about His Wonderful Nature.

And this Jesus Christ *is* alive!

And anyone who is alive, and near us, has an effect on us. Jesus Christ is alive and near you (*in* you!) as you sit reading your Bible, and if you will read it with an open mind, being willing to admit to some interest now and then, He will light up your mind and little by little it will begin to clear up for you. None of us will ever understand all that's in the Holy Bible. God's Mind is so great we couldn't begin to keep up with it. And don't forget, the Bible is God's Book. So, don't put it down and quit just because you get stuck and can't understand something. Don't even *try* to figure it out. Just keep reading and stay open. Read it and ask the Holy Spirit to give you the impression He wants you to have as you read it.

Read a chapter of one of the Gospels straight through and then think back on it. Or just sit there in the quiet with God and let it soak into your subconscious. Even if your conscious mind does *not* grasp what you read, EVERYTHING you read and hear drops into your *subconscious* mind and it will be there for your use maybe years later!

Can you ever learn to *like* to read the Bible?

Yes, because Christ is alive and He will draw your interest to the story of Himself in the Bible, *if* you are willing to be drawn!

The Bible is about Him, and He did come out of that tomb!

Is there anything dull about that?

8

How Can I Love Someone I Can't See?

"I can understand my *friend's* loving me, but I can't see or touch Jesus, so it's hard to understand about His loving me.

"How can I love someone I can't even see?"

This may sound like a very childlike question, but it is one that stabs at the back of the minds of as many so-called adults as young people! I'm glad you asked this question. It's one of the best in the entire list. A very old lady asked me not long ago: "Genie, don't you think the hardest part about being a Christian is that we can't *see* God?"

Well, certainly that fact can be one of the most confusing and discouraging things about being a Christian. But I believe you'll agree after we've thought this through together for a few minutes, that the very fact that we cannot now *see* God *can* be one of the most exciting and stimulating things about Christianity! You may not agree with that now, but I hope you have your mind opened up to the possibility that I might have a point. Remember, I'm writing to you out of my own experience. This isn't coming out of someone else's book!

I've tried it.

When I first became a Christian, I didn't love God. I had simply been made aware that something had to be done! Time spent with my friend, Ellen, in whose life Jesus Christ was Master, made me see how far off-center I was and how wrong and selfish and out of tune with everything! I had not really believed in God before at all. And there I was confronted with a fact which I had always considered colorful tradition and nothing more! Ellen said Jesus Christ was God come to earth in the form of a Man, who died on a Cross in order that He should Himself be the bridge over which I could walk back into my Heavenly Father's house. I hadn't believed in the Heavenly Father for eighteen years; and maybe before that, when I was a child, I only thought I believed in Him because my family did. But as soon as I was exposed to this *Living Christ* through her, I began to feel uncomfortable and jealous.

Uncomfortable because I felt so out of tune with life.

Uncomfortable because I was so jittery and nervous and tied in knots.

Uncomfortable because suddenly down under the level of my conscious mind, there seemed to be stirring a conviction that there might be a God after all, and that if so He was a complete Stranger to me!

Uncomfortable because suddenly I felt a black, yawning space between this God and me—a space I couldn't possibly reach across!

Uncomfortable and afraid because I felt lost.

Lost from the self God intended me to be, and lost from God.

I felt all of these things because I had literally been exposed to the Presence of the Living Christ in this loyal little disciple of His! It was not what she said to me. It was the fact that I *knew* she belonged to Someone else who would take care of her. I only belonged to myself and I was afraid—alone!

I knew I couldn't really take care of myself, no matter how much I had always boasted that I could!

I was uncomfortable, mildly speaking, for these reasons and more.

But I was also jealous.

Jealous of what she had.

Jealous of Who had her!

Jealous of the peace in her eyes.

Jealous of the fact that she seemed always about to break into a smile as though she knew a big, shining secret!

Jealous of this Secret!

Jealous of her apparent inner poise.

Jealous because she had kept her looks through the years with Christ and I had not! (He can restore the years the locusts have eaten, though, if someone over twenty-five happens to be reading this!)

Jealous of the fact that she said she simply did not *need* to drink or smoke anymore and that I knew she said it because it was true! She had resources for anything. The Resources of God.

While I was becoming more and more uncomfortable and more and more jealous, I became more and more alone. I felt as though I were a third party!

Have you ever been a "third party"? Have you ever gone out with a couple very much in love—but you didn't even have a friend with you? Maybe you were with your brother and his girl, or your sister and her boyfriend. You felt so alone and unwanted and you ached inside for someone to love you and pay attention to *you!*

You were so aware of how much *they* loved each other.

This may seem like a poor example. But the first thing that made me want what Ellen had in Christ was the fact that she was so sure that He loved her! And although I couldn't understand it at all, I found myself being sure that she loved Him! And I felt like a "third party."

She had the greatest capacity for human love I had ever seen, but even though I would have said I didn't even believe in a Personal God, I was completely sure that Jesus Christ *was* her Beloved!

And that she was His!

She didn't obey Him because she feared Him. She obeyed Him because she loved Him.

I knew she couldn't *see* Him! But I knew she loved Him.

I didn't want to believe it, but I had to! There it was.

Six weeks later, as I've already told you, He was *my* Saviour, too, but I must be honest and say that Christ did not become my *Beloved* until after I had known Him as my Saviour for awhile. This makes sense, doesn't it? And it leads us directly to the answer to the question at the beginning of this chapter: "How can I love someone I can't even see?"

Well, although you may not understand it right off, the answer is in another of the writings of John, this one called First John, in the fourth chapter, the ninth and tenth verses: "The love of God . . . exists in this, *not that we loved God, but that He loved us* and sent His Son as an atoning sacrifice for our sins."

Now, with your mind wide open, catch hold of that phrase ". . . not that we loved God, but that *He loved us* . . . ." Got it? If you have, you're holding the key to how you can love God even though you can't see Him! And the key is this: just as you open your mind to receive a new fact you are about to learn in school, or when you're reading a book, do the same thing with your heart. Open your *heart* toward the love of God and see what happens!

No sparks will fly and the sun won't change color, but a tiny flame will begin to burn in your heart and the ice will begin to melt! If you are willing to expose yourself to God's Love for you, by accepting His Gift of Eternal Life which He holds out to everyone who receives Jesus Christ as his or her *personal Saviour, you will begin to love God in return!*

How do I know?

Because I tried it and because life proves it. The Love of God is worked out in lesser degree in human beings but the same laws apply. By that I mean this: a child does not love its mother *until* it becomes aware of how much the mother loves the child! Did you know that? When you were first born, you didn't love your mother. You had the *capacity* for love built right into your very being, but *until*, in the simplest way, you began to experience your mother's love for you as she fed you, bathed you, smiled at you and caressed you in her arms, *you had no response to her love at all.* We learn to love when we have first been exposed to the love of another. Love breeds love.

Love is contagious, as smiles are contagious. If you're feeling in the pink as you ride along on a streetcar and you begin to smile at someone who looks glum, you can usually bring a smile out of that person because *you* hold the higher of the two emotions—love. Love and good will are more powerful than hate and ill will. A smile is more powerful than a frown.

Using the example of mother and child again, the baby doesn't smile until he or she "catches on" *how* to smile from mother smiling down into the cradle day after day. Not long ago, someone told me about a three-year-old boy, who, although he was perfectly normal mentally, seldom spoke at all. Usually three-year-olds seldom stop chattering. This little fellow went about his play in silence for the most part. Why? Because his mother never talked to him!

I think you have the general idea now, haven't you?

". . . not that we loved God, but that *He loved us* . . . !"

The Bible tells us in this same book (First John) that actually *God is love.* He is the very source of love. Just as a river has a source — a place from which it springs first, so all love (if it is real love) springs from God Himself. His very Nature is Love. And when God comes to dwell within us in the Person of the Holy Spirit, we have the very springs of love right there inside us!

Are you beginning to see that we need not, we *cannot* cook up love toward God by our own efforts? He doesn't expect us to. He just says through Jesus Christ, "Come to Me" and I'll love you into loving Me!

Will you let Jesus Christ love you all He wants to? Will you?

9

How Can I Actually Walk with God?

"What does it mean to walk with God?"
"What does worshiping God really mean?"

A girl said to me not long ago, "Well, Genie, I can walk home from school with John, my boy-friend, but how can I walk with God? I'm not trying to dodge walking with God, I just don't get what it means!"

She wrapped it all up in a neat little package. There would be many more like this girl, who would walk with God if they knew what it really means; many who would worship God if they didn't have worship associated *only* with going to church once a week. If we can just lay hold of the exciting, transforming fact that worshiping God and walking with God could actually "light up" our ordinary, daily lives, more and more of us would begin at once to walk with Him.

Mel Trotter, the famous evangelist, once said that he never knew *anyone* who didn't at least *like* Jesus Christ! That's a big statement. And he included atheists, Jews, Hindus, Christians, non-Christians—everyone. Whether or not someone believes Jesus Christ is the Living Son of God, nevertheless, down deep in every man and woman is a kind of *response* to the Personality of Jesus. They respect Him, at least. Try asking anyone who denies Him if he or she believes Jesus was lying when He was here on this earth!

I've never yet found *anyone* who would *dare* say, "Yes, He lied."

Something built right into the fibre of our beings reveres the very Name of Jesus Christ! This, of course, is because God created us to belong to Himself and He was in Christ and *is* One with Christ. Even those who flatly deny that Jesus of Nazareth was any more than a great teacher, will hedge and try to change the subject if you ask them if they think Jesus ever lied outright or was dead wrong!

You may find someone who will say He lied, or was wrong, but having tried to say it once myself, back in the days when I believed I was an atheist, I can tell you it makes the heart beat like a sledge hammer with a healthy kind of fear of what you've said!

This is not superstition or someone else's conscience imposed upon you. This is simply true because Jesus Christ and God *are* One, and Jesus is alive and is constantly trying to draw all men unto Himself.

Even if your friend laughs when you mention that

you love Jesus Christ and follow Him in your daily life, just keep on loving your friend and don't mind the laugh. It's mainly because the mention of Jesus makes human beings nervous. When you mention Jesus or even when you do not mention His Name, if you are allowing Him to live His Own Life *in* you, just your calm, well-adjusted Christian personality points your non-Christian friends to His actual Presence and they squirm or laugh or make a gag to cover up their nervousness. This isn't hard to understand because if you are a Christian, God Himself is standing there right *in* you. Not because you're a perfect Christian, but because God gave you the Gift of Himself when you received Him!

People may toss off the mention of *God.*

Few, if any, are indifferent to *Jesus Christ.* God, if He is *not defined* in the Person of Jesus, with the Purity and Strength and Courage and Kindness and Redeeming Power of Jesus Christ, can be *anything* to anyone. He can be a long pink blur, in fact. Or a nameless Force. But mention Jesus Christ, and God becomes definite and His claims upon our lives become clear. Jesus Christ said we were to forsake all and follow Him! This stops people short in their tracks. They can't ignore Him. They can refuse Him, but no one can be truly indifferent about Jesus Christ!

Church can be ignored.

The *Bible* can be put on the shelf.

But Jesus Christ came *out* of that tomb. He's alive! And He just stands there confronting the world with Himself, saying, "I loved you enough to die for you . . . come unto Me!"

He is impossible to ignore.

He can be rejected.

But He cannot be *ignored,* once He has had a chance to make His claim on a human life, however that claim may be made!

You may be wondering what this has to do with "walking with God." You may be wondering what it has to do with worship.

Just this: He brings about a reaction in *everyone* because He is alive! Even those who appear to be indifferent to Him, use His Name when they want to concoct an oath that is particularly strong! I know this from my own experience before my conversion. If anyone had asked me about Jesus Christ, I would have laughed or sworn—using His Name, most likely, to make my statement stand out!

That's just what Jesus Christ does! *He stands out!*

And I have come to believe that everyone who uses His Name as profanity, uses it because of a deep down subconscious longing for Jesus Christ!

You may not have thought of that. I believe it.

And so just as Jesus Christ brings about definite reactions and responses in those who hate Him or do *not* follow Him, so He brings about *definite* reactions and responses among those of us who *are* His followers.

The extent of our worship is in direct proportion to our *reaction* and *response* to Jesus Christ! This, of course, is true in friendships among those we know. If we really love someone, we respond to him or to her! If we really love someone, we—react favorably. If we really love God, we respond and react to Him. We worship Him.

Walking with your friend is very, very much like walking with God in one big way—you are being *with* your friend when you walk together and you are being *with* God when you walk with Him. But we all know that we cannot *have* a friend until we have agreed to *be* friends with that friend. Maybe we don't actually take a vow of friendship, but we do experience a time when we "receive" the friendship of one certain person and then another. Something that is unseen about that friend, something of that friend's soul and heart and mind and spirit and personality comes over into your soul and heart and mind and spirit and personality. When you take someone's hand, you give your hand at the same time, don't you? When you smile at your friend, "something" unseen, but very, very *real* passes between you. This "something" goes *into* your being from your friend's being and into your friend's being from yours!

Another question which I was asked can be answered here: "What does it mean to *receive* Jesus Christ into my life?"

It means receiving the Spirit of Christ right into your very being. It literally means "receiving" His Friendship! Just as you receive your earthly friend's love and friendship, so you can receive the Love and Friendship of God.

We can believe that He meant what He said and receive Him as our Saviour from sin, whether or not we know or understand Him. We can believe that Jesus Christ died for our sins and rose from the dead and we can step right out in faith and act on it by receiving Him as our Saviour so that we become Christians, just as simply as we can step right over to the light switch on the wall and snap the light on, even though we don't understand electricity and even though we didn't *know* Benjamin Franklin as a close friend!

Then, after we have received Jesus as our Saviour, we begin to "walk" with Him and we *want* to worship Him. He then becomes our Friend. We worship as we walk with Him, because in every colored leaf and stone, every whirling red star in every moon-white night, every time that "certain person" laughs or smiles, every time the rain smells as it smells on summer sidewalks and in every flash of sunlight on a fighting trout . . . in the good crack of ball on bat . . . even in music so sweet it makes you want to cry . . . even in tears, we will find Christ!

If we belong to Him.

About sixty-three years after the Lord Jesus left the earth, after He broke right out of that dark sealed tomb, and ascended into heaven, the Apostle Paul wrote this to the people who got together to start the first Christian church in a place called Colossae: ". . . As you did accept Christ Jesus as Lord, live *in union with Him,* rooted and built up *in* Him and confirmed *in* the faith . . ." This quotation is from the Berkeley Version of the New Testament, and you will notice that the familiar word "walk" is translated "live in union with Him."

How Can I Actually Walk with God?

So, if we bring the ancient use of the word "walk" up-to-date, as Dr. Verkuyl does in his translation of the New Testament, we can easily see that to "walk with Him" simply means to "live in *union* with Him." We all know that if we have done something wrong and sinful, we cannot stay close to Jesus. We want to get away from Him and hide! And to stay in *union* means to be one with Him, so that if we really *walk* with God, we see to it that if we do sin, we turn at once and ask forgiveness so that we can be restored to that *union* with Christ just as soon as possible! And "just as soon as possible" is immediately—in less than a split second, since our forgiveness is available because of the fact that Jesus has already died and shed His Own Blood for us! We become one again with God because of what Jesus did, when we ask forgiveness in His Name. It's like being able to sign His Name to a check!

It's also like having a letter or a note from someone big and important so you can "get in" when others can't! But when we see what this Free Pass into the Presence of the Father cost Jesus on the Cross, we lose all our desire to sin because we love Him so much we don't want to take advantage of Anyone who did so much for us!

Worshiping God in everything we do, walking with Him, or being in union with Him, means that HE IS WITH US WHEREVER WE GO. We are in contact with Christ. This is the best way to find out what a Christian can and cannot do. We don't need religious laws to live by! We have God living right in us, and He is alive, so He will let you know beyond the shadow of any doubt *if* you will listen to Him, whether or not He is happy at the party or the entertainment to which the TWO OF YOU have gone together! Just because you choose to disobey Him and go someplace where He would not feel "at home," does not mean that God *stays* at home! He goes right with you. And every few minutes, He will press against your heart and your heart will ache because you know His Heart aches over your disobedience.

Walking with Him simply means *living* with Him.

10

Why Is Sex Wrong If God Made It?

"If God made us with sex emotions, why does the Bible say it's wrong?"

A straightforward question deserves a straightforward answer. The Bible does *not* say "sex is wrong"!

God did make our sex urges. They are a part of the drive that makes for creative, joyful, constructive living. And the Bible does not say sex is a sin at all.

Sex is not a sin.

But what we do with sex can be a sin!

To have a desire to express yourself is not sin. But if you express yourself in certain ways which are not in tune with the rest of God's creation—that self expression becomes sin. Now, before we go into this, let's get this one point clear: God created you, gave you a free will, and put you down in a *moral* universe to live out a certain number of years. When I say God created a *moral* universe, this is what I mean: He built right into the fabric of the universe a certain spiritual and moral Plan. It would be more accurate to say God created the universe a certain way and when we go *against* the grain of the universe, we crash right up against what appear to be *unbreakable* laws! Universal moral laws.

The Bible lays down certain signposts for us and if we observe these as a pattern for living, we will live *with* the grain of God's universe and not bang ourselves up against this unbreakable Plan.

If you stop to think about it, you can't break God's universal laws!

That's what I said. You can't break God's laws. They're unbreakable. But you can break *yourself over* those laws!

Did you ever snap a piece of kindling wood over your knee when you're building a wood fire? That's exactly what you do with your life when you insist upon disobeying God. It isn't God who breaks you. You break yourself. God isn't *after* you with a stick! But you can break yourself just like a stick of dry wood, if you decide to play God and make your own pattern for living.

Let's say it again: God's Plan is unbreakable.

Whether you or I *like* His Plan is beside the point. You may say, "How do you expect me to love a God who is so tough?" I don't expect you to love a tough God. God isn't tough. He's wiser than we are, that's all. He can see the whole picture of our lives. He is very concerned with your every minute, but He is also concerned

with your every year ahead on this earth and all the way
into eternity! He is so concerned, in fact, that He knows
ignoring just *one* of His signposts might permit you to do
something (just for fun or pleasure!) which could spoil
God's highest Plan for all the rest of your life! I don't
mean God won't forgive you if you sin. That isn't what I
said. But although we are creatures of free will and *can*
choose whether we will obey God or run our own wild and
wobbly courses, we *cannot* choose the consequences of
our choices!

Did you get that?

We can choose what we will do—but we *cannot*
choose the consequences of our choices! When we disobey God, misuse a gift of His, such as our sex drives and
emotions, then we bring the consequences of our choice
crashing down upon our own heads! God doesn't pick out
a set of "consequences" and send them to you for punish-
ment. He created you and He created the universe, and
life as He created it just will not back up a lie or a will-
ful sin against God!

And I repeat, God did not make the universe and
you in this particular way because He wanted to be difficult. He made it this way because He knew nothing
else would work! Jesus Christ was there at creation according to the very first part of the Gospel of John, and
so the teachings of Jesus Christ are laid down according
to the Plan which was built right into the universe. That
is why a life lived in obedience to the Lord Jesus works—
and a life lived *against* Him does not work in the final
analysis. If you are not obeying God you may think your

life is working fine now. But it will break itself eventually over the very Plan of Creation!

If God had known any other plan would be better, He would have brought it into existence. The Bible tells us what God's idea is, however, and even though many, many people *do* disagree, that doesn't in any way change the fact that God is God and we are really pretty silly to be disagreeing with Him!

I doubt that the most conceited person you know is conceited enough to say he or she is wiser than God, do you?

Now, back to our question: "If God made us with sex emotions, why does the Bible say it's wrong?" The Bible says that certain sexual behaviour is wrong—simply because the Bible is God's Holy Word and God knows what works out for happiness and He also knows what works out for trouble and heartbreak! Over and over and over I want to remind you that God has a *reason* for everything. He did not sit down on some distant white throne and think up all the unpleasant things for you to do, and mark off all the pleasant ones! He is working with the *whole picture* of mankind, remember. And He has a Purpose in all of this creation of His which no one on this earth will ever fully know. If a member of your family has gone ahead to be with God, he or she knows all these unanswered questions about creation now. He or she knows God's full Purpose. But he wants *us* to follow and obey Him on this earth because we have faith and confidence in Him as a Person, and not because we understand it all. Yes, God created sex, and part of the reason

He did is so that the world could be populated with new people to take the place of those who have lived out their life span on this earth. But remember, I said this is only part of the reason.

I fully believe that God had other purposes in creating the sex drive within us all. When a man and woman are married, and the marriage is consecrated by God, surely there could be no earthly joy and no pleasure more wonderful than the sex relationship between these two who have been joined together in spirit as well as in body, by the God who created them and who died for them. But, the happy Christian married couples whom I know . . . the ones who are truly in love with each other, look upon the sex act *only* as a means of further expression of their love and perhaps of further creation if God wills to give them a child of their love. It is quite possible and not at all uncommon for a Christian married couple to become too centered on the physical side of their life! Just because they are married does not give them the right to put *anything* above their love of God. They can become centered in each other and neglect their Christian lives; neglect God because they are concentrating upon each other when they ordinarily would have been spending time with God.

I am bringing this point up because most of you will be married one day, and I truly believe that sex emotions can rule us wrongly if we are married as well as single. In other words, again—not just because a specific law is written down in God's Word do we obey it, but because it is another key to a balanced, happy life.

Don't feel that God is gypping you because you can't give free rein to your sex desires!

Free rein to your sex emotions does not mean self-expression! It means self-*ruin!* You may declare yourself free to do as you please, but do you know what you are free to do? You are free to get into trouble!

Only when we *obey* God's Plan are we really free.

I have found to my great surprise and delight that the *only freedom* there is in the universe as God created it is in *obedience to God!*

If you really think this out, you won't be angry at God because of it. You'll realize that it's all because He's God and we're *not!* If you knew best for you and I knew best for me, what kind of a helter-skelter world would we have?

If God had *not* built absolute laws right into the very warp and woof of the universe, we would be in a perpetual state of complete confusion! I for one am glad this is a dependable universe, aren't you?

I do hope that in thinking of the subject of sex emotions you will open your mind to something which few people are wise enough to see. I hope *you* are wise enough to get hold of this: Sex, as God created it, is *not only* for birth and pleasure! I am convinced from my own life and from the lives of others who have never married, that the original plan for the sex drives in our beings swings far out beyond those two points, to take in the whole creative side of life!

It is natural and normal to want sex fulfillment. But it is neither promised by God nor necessary, according to His Plan, that we find that fulfillment in physical relations with another person. God does not promise a happy married life, but He does promise an "abundant life"; and knowing the kind of God He is, I can't imagine that He would say He came to give me, a single Christian woman, "an abundant life" if He didn't mean that it *could* be that way! I know He meant it—because my life is full to overflowing, and the world is well populated with happy, radiant, fulfilled, busy, creative Christian men and women who are *not* married.

Most likely you will be married. I believe God has a Plan for every life. Usually that Plan includes a mate and a home and a family. I mention the fulfillment of the Christian *single* life, mainly to point out to you that the sex emotions are not as limited as we would make them.

But most of all, remember this . . . sex is not wrong. The Bible does not say sex is a sin. *The Bible says certain wrong uses of sex separate us from God, and anything that separates us from God is sin.* God knows you so well. Knows what makes you tick. Knows that if you get centered on a sexual attraction you might miss the real thing when it comes along! Because, get this . . . if you are attracted to someone for the pleasure that person gives *you*, that is not love. Not the kind of love on which you can build a marriage. Attraction centered in sex breaks down! Love builds up! Sex attraction thinks of what pleases *you*. Real love thinks of what pleases the other person!

Let God guide you into the *real thing*, will you?

Don't take matters into your own hands. He knows much more about love than you do.

11

Why Do I Have to Pray If God Knows Everything?

"If God knows everything already, why do I have to pray in order to tell Him about what I want and need?"

"How do I learn to pray so that God hears and answers my prayers?"

My prayer-life has been the weakest part of my Christian life. I have a notion this would be true of many people if they dared to admit it, don't you? We hear people pray who use long, flowery phrases which sound high and mighty, but somehow so often I don't get a sense of high enough to *reach* the Almighty!

Prayer isn't so much *what* we say, but what's in our hearts and our minds *as we say it!* Prayer isn't so much what we say as *whose* we are while we pray!

Prayer, of course, in order for God to be *able* to answer it, must be "in the Will of God." And that raises a question that rings a bell (or a buzzer!) in the mind of almost everyone:

HOW CAN WE KNOW THE WILL OF GOD?

Some will ask, "Can we really know the Will of God?"

As my friend, Mary Welch, says in her very excellent and easy to understand book called *Hands of Prayer* "[we certainly can know the Will of God] otherwise Jesus would not have said, 'I give you the keys of the kingdom.'" Jesus meant every word He said and He said *so many* dynamic, power-packed things about prayer!

First of all, when His disciples asked Him, "Lord, teach us to pray," He gave them a model prayer which we now know as the Lord's Prayer. We've all said this so many times it has come to be just a jumble of words linked together in a sort of rhythm which groups of people fall into when they repeat something aloud together. I suggest that you stop right now (or just as soon as you have time) and repeat the Lord's Prayer aloud, really *thinking* about each word. Ask the Holy Spirit to give you some new light on what the Lord's Prayer really means.

Before we get anywhere with prayer, we must believe that it *is possible* to know the Will of God in every small *and* large situation that comes up. When I pray now, I try to realize that the Holy Spirit is really praying through me, *in* the Will of God. The Bible tells us that when *we* don't know how to pray, the Spirit does know, because He knows God's Will exactly, since He *is* God. So, when you pray, picture a connection from God, through the "conductor," the Holy Spirit, to your mind and heart. *God's Will comes along this line to you.* You pray for the thing which is *in* God's Will, according to the prompting of the Holy Spirit within you. Then He transmits the message back to Jesus Christ (who is alive forever to intercede or take our requests to the Father), and then Jesus Himself takes up this prayer in your behalf and presents the whole thing to the Father! And we must remember this: the Father *wants to answer your prayer which is prayed in His Will and in the Name of Jesus Christ.*

Read back through that paragraph again and be sure you have the picture straight about the route *real* prayer takes! It begins in the Mind of God. The Holy Spirit puts it *into* our minds. We send it *back* through the Holy Spirit, who transmits it to Jesus Christ. Jesus Christ sits at the right Hand of the Father making intercession for us every minute. Then Jesus Himself, still our burden-bearer, takes our prayer requests right into the Presence of the Father—who *wants* to answer them!

One big way the Father shows His love for us is at the point where He answers our prayers. There are two sides to the love that is between God and us. One side is our request, the other side is God's loving response! Like two halves of an apple, they fit together to make a whole. Jesus described this wonderful two-way process of prayer in Matthew 7:7, 8 when He said: "Keep on asking, and the gift will be given you; keep on seeking, and you will find; keep on knocking, and the door will open to you. For everyone who keeps on asking, receives, and everyone who keeps on seeking, finds, and to the one who keeps on knocking, the door will open."* The King James version of the Bible says: *"Ask* and it shall be *given . . . seek* and ye shall *find,* etc." Do you see the two parts fitting together?

However this does not go for *anything* we want!

And right about here someone will say, "But, Genie, what about Jesus' promise in Mark 11:24:—'. . . whenever you pray and ask for *anything,* have faith that it has been granted you, and you will get it'—doesn't this say anything?"*

Yes, it does. But it also says "have faith that it has been *granted* to you." Do you think for one minute that God would *grant* an answer to a prayer that would end up making you sin? For example, if you pray for a date with someone whom you *know* will be an influence against your Christian life,—or who will tempt you to disobey God,—do you think God would be foolish enough to grant that request? You may get the date, but it won't be God giving it to you!

Here is another more exaggerated example: If you are so angry with someone that you want to beat him up, do you think God would answer your prayer to give you a whack at that person in a dark alley alone?

Be very wary of taking one line out of the Bible and of twisting it to come out the way *you* want it to come out! We all have to be careful of that. And Jesus, in John 14:13 makes it very clear that we are to pray in *His Name,* which means *in His Nature!* He says: ". . . I will bring about whatever you ask in My name, so that

* The New Testament, translated by Charles B. Williams. Copyright assigned 1949 to the Moody Bible Institute of Chicago. Used by permission.

the Father may be glorified in the Son." Could you ask for an opportunity to sin in the Name of Jesus? If you ask for a chance to do something which you know will hurt God, do you think that would *glorify* Him? And didn't Jesus say He would answer prayer so that "the Father may be glorified"?

It is not just the sign-off of a prayer—"We ask these things in the Name of the Lord Jesus"—that brings God's answer. It is the prayer itself and the intent of your heart as you pray!

After all, when someone says, "You may use my name," that means that the person whose name is important enough for you to want to use, *knows* that you won't *misuse* his name. And the only way we can be sure we are not *mis*using the Name of Jesus, is to live in absolute union with Him. To walk with Him. To abide with and in Him and He in us! Like the vine and the branches in Chapter 15 of the Gospel of John. Read it and make a picture in your mind of the word-picture Jesus painted when He said He is the Vine and we are the branches who live *growing onto* Him!

The first question at the beginning of this chapter asks: "If God knows everything already, why do I have to pray in order to tell Him about what I want and need?"

This is a good question—right to the heart of the matter.

There are three definite answers which come to me.

(1) Prayer is, in its highest sense, *being with God.* How long would a friendship or a romance last if you never spoke to the person you loved? How long would

it last or how deep would its roots grow if you never *listened* to the other person? One of the secrets of a prayer life that really counts is that we spend time in the silence, just listening to the still small Voice of God within us, prompting us to do this and that. After all, if you go to a doctor, you don't spout forth your complaints and run out of his office, shouting, "Help me, Doctor, help me!" You tell him what's wrong and then you sit and listen to what he tells you to do in order to get well! The same goes when you are talking to God. He's a Person too. So, prayer *does* deepen our Friendship with God. The more time we spend with someone the better we know him, don't forget.

(2) A second answer has to do with *surrender.* Unless the Holy Spirit is in full possession of *you,* and has room to move about and work within you—that is, unless *you give* Him that room, by not demanding *your* way in everything, He cannot properly communicate between you and God, the Father. Do you remember the picture we imagined of the Holy Spirit as a conductor or a transmitter between you and the Father, through Jesus Christ? Well, it stands to reason, doesn't it, that unless this Messenger has the freedom of your *entire* life, the message He takes to Christ about you will *not* be clear because you are not clear! You are blocking the whole exciting plan somewhere along the line because you are being stubborn on one point or another. And so, prayer, in order to be answered, must be taken to God in a clear, pure form. If you spend time in prayer, the Holy Spirit will teach you these things. Jesus promised that. *They do not come overnight.*

— 89 —

(3) A third reason for prayer is so that we can keep score on God! Make your prayers *definite*. Don't just plead, "Oh, God, *if* I have sinned, forgive me." Examine yourself and tell God the definite places where you *know* you have sinned . . . where you have pushed your own will or opinion or where you refused to obey your parents, or *tell* God that you didn't speak to someone at school today, and ask His forgiveness. Make your *needs definite*. If you need a new coat (remember I said *"need"*) say, "Father, I think I need a new coat. If You give it to me I shall be grateful, but if You don't think I need it, I will love You just as much anyway." If He thinks you need it, *you'll get it*, if you believe. And if you have made your prayers definite, you can keep score on the answers and the more answers you can record, the more your faith in God will grow. If you pray for patience, don't be surprised if God sends along a relative who is cross and gets on your nerves! That will be so that you can *learn* patience! So, put it down as an answer to prayer. And when you get to the place where you can play a game of Life with God like this, you will find that you have been given a brand new sense of humor too! So that's another reason for prayer!

There comes a day, after we have spent enough time in the Presence of God, when we find ourselves praying mostly for other people. You see, the reason for this is that after we have "walked" with God long enough to be moving *with the current* of His Love and living *with the grain* of His universe, we don't need to ask much for ourselves. It isn't that we want less, it's that we *have so much!*

None of this is possible overnight, so don't be impatient. I hope you have learned as much from reading this chapter as I learned from consulting with the Lord Jesus as I wrote it. I expect my own prayer-life to be better from now on because we have shared this chapter on prayer. So, I thank you so much for asking those questions. You made me think too! From now on let's begin to look at prayer as the exciting adventure with God that it really is. Will you do that *with me?*

12

Why Do We Have to Suffer If God Loves Us

"Why do we have to suffer if God loves us?"

"If God is Love, why does He let such terrible things happen to people? How about the little children who were burned in an overheated trailer? How about the old people who were burned when that rest home caught fire? They were all innocent like the children who got killed! Where is God in all this?"

"How does God comfort a Christian in time of sorrow and trouble? What does He do? The trouble is still there, isn't it?"

I have seen people so grief stricken that they hated God.

Some tragedies are so ghastly . . . some trouble is so deep . . . some problems seem so hopeless, that the human heart, even when it tries to follow God, can reach the point where it cries, "Why did You create us in the first place?"

"Why?"

Why Do We Have to Suffer If God Loves Us?

Now, this may seem a strange subject for this book. But if young people are exempt from death and heartache and suffering, it's news to me! Some of the most courageous, really victorious people I know are teen-agers who have gone through their times of testing like the true disciples of Christ that they are!

No one is excused from suffering.

It comes at different times to different people and in different ways. But if we love, we must eventually suffer, because loss is keener, just as companionship is keener, when we love. There is an old East Indian proverb which says the deeper sorrow carves its way into our beings, the more joy we can contain. You may not think joy is worth knowing sorrow first. But whether you think it is or not, sorrow will come to us all sooner or later in one form or another.

This is not being pessimistic.

This is not being a kill-joy.

This is simply facing facts as they are. No one is excused from physical death in this life, and if we love anyone at all anywhere, we are going to know grief when that person dies. This need not depress us at all. Jesus knew grief. Do you remember when He found out that His dear friend Lazarus had died, that Jesus wept? So grief is natural. We needn't lose any sleep lying awake wondering what we are going to do when trouble strikes our lives, because there is something much better we can do.

We can be prepared for it.

I have a close friend named Mary Webster who saw her husband killed right in front of her eyes in an automobile accident. Mary really knew Jesus, although she had only been a Christian about a year. And she took Jesus at His Word that her husband, Roy, was *not* dead, but eternally alive at that moment, and Mary went through her tragedy victoriously. Of course, she missed her husband. But Mary believed Jesus meant it when He promised Eternal Life, and she determined right there in the middle of the road, before any help had come to the scene of the accident, that she would walk *through* the tragedy *with* Christ! She was prepared to take Him at His Word. When we *believe* something it means we are willing to *act* as though we believe it!

Mary Webster has tried this out. And her word to all of us who still have a tragedy up ahead is this:

"We must all be modern Noahs! The flood is coming, so we might just as well have our arks ready."

Mary knows that more tragedy is ahead of her too.

She *is* prepared to take her own advice and be ready.

So am I. I have faced before God the worst that I can imagine happening to me. I have told Him that I would accept it if it comes. I will not fight it. I will accept it and trust Him to take me through it and out the other side victoriously!

Does this sound like a lot of Pollyanna stuff to you?

Not practical?

Maybe not even *possible?*

Do you feel, as I always felt before I was a Christian, that if your parents or your best friend or your sweetheart should die that you would either lie down on the church floor at the funeral and kick and scream or throw something at the minister standing up there saying things about God being the Great Comforter in time of sorrow?

I felt that way until I met Jesus Christ and began to catch onto the fact that God has something *very definite and practical to say in suffering.* That although we may not understand on this earth *why* some particular thing happened as it did, God does have an answer. More than that, He *is* the Answer.

What does that mean?

The first question you asked is this: "If God is Love, why does He let such terrible things happen to people?" And then this question goes on to list two tragedies which I remember reading about in the papers. Two small children were burned (one killed) when their family's overheated trailer caught fire. I remember the shudder that went all through me when I read of the frantic cries of the helpless old people who were burned (some fatally) when the frame rest home in which they lived caught fire in the middle of the night! These are striking examples of real tragedy! The question is a deep one. One I cannot answer completely. No one can. But knowing something of the Character and Heart of God, as He revealed Himself in the Person of Jesus Christ, I cannot accept for one instant the fact that this same God who let His Own Heart break on a Cross of Supreme Pain in order to *save* us, would ever *will* any tragedy!

God has a permissive will which permits even sin. We cannot understand why this is. We just know that it is. There are many things too deep and too high for our understanding. Why God ever permitted sin to enter the

NEVER A DULL MOMENT

world, since He is all Powerful, no one can say for certain. But one day we will know His entire Purpose; for now, we have His Character and His Word on which to hang all our hopes. So, God did not *send* those tragedies, but His permissive will *allowed* them.

And if you are about to ask "why" let me ask you to think through these things I am about to say to you.

Let's take two examples. First, let's take the accident in which my friend's husband was killed. Mary and Roy had two wonderful young sons. Mary and her husband loved each other deeply. They had a fine farm, and Roy's sister, Aunt May, lived with them. They were a very happy family. Surely a farmer's wife needs her husband to run the farm! Surely Aunt May loved her brother! Surely those two boys, Claudie and Teddy, needed a father! Why did God allow this to happen?

The answer is simple.

God created an *orderly universe*. Remember we said we can depend upon God's laws working at all times? We can depend upon the law of gravity. And we can also depend upon the laws governing *motion*. On a country road at a certain moment, just as the Webster family car approached a certain place in the road, the steering gear locked on a big trailer truck barreling down toward them from the opposite direction! When the helpless driver could no longer steer the truck, the big trailer broke loose and since it was *in motion*, it *followed the law governing motion until it hit an object which slowed and then stopped it*. This object was the Webster family car, and Roy Webster was killed. We call this tragedy, and it is.

But suppose God had suspended those physical laws in order to protect the Webster family, what would have happened to every other object in the universe which happened to be in motion at that instant? God cannot make cosmic pets of Christians. If a Christian's child leans too far over a second-story balcony, he is going to fall, because if God suspended the law of gravity for this one child, everything on the face of the earth would begin to move around because gravity is a pull toward the center of the earth. It holds us in place.

This does not mean that God cannot and does not perform miracles. He does. And we cannot anticipate or know why He does at some times and not at others. We can't know this because we can only see a small part of the entire Plan of Creation right now. But we can trust God to know what He's doing, and our part is to be willing to accept, *without feeling sorry for ourselves*, anything that comes to us. What if Jesus had felt sorry for Himself when they drove the first nail into His outstretched Hand? If His Heart had been chocked with self-pity as He hung there on the Cross suffering for our sakes, He couldn't have smothered our sin in His Heart. There wouldn't have been room for it. It would have been full of His Own self-pity!

Now take the example of the fire in the overheated trailer or the rest home. I believe sin caused both fires. Is this God's fault? The trailer was allowed to get overheated through ignorance or carelessness, and yet I know thousands of people wondered how *God* could have let it happen! The rest home was an old frame building. Faulty wiring, as I remember, caused the fire. Isn't it *careless* to allow helpless old people to live in an old frame building with faulty electrical wiring? And isn't carelessness sin? Yes, God *allows* sin. He surely doesn't *will* it, but He has some reason for *permitting* it. It is tied up with our free will. We can always *choose* to sin. But the Holy Spirit always gives us the power *not* to sin. So, when *our sin* causes tragedy, it is foolish to blame God!

I am not saying that all tragedy results from sin. Some tragedy is unexplainable. Our part is to look squarely at God and follow His example when He Himself faced the worst tragedy that could befall anyone—the Cross of Calvary!

He did *not* pity Himself as we so often do.

He hung there and said in the midst of His Suffering . . . "Father forgive them . . ."

He took the "world's supreme tragedy and turned it into the world's supreme victory!" He *saved us* through *His sorrow* and *suffering*. He made full *use* of His Tragedy. And if He is the kind of God I believe Him to be, He will *also* show *us* a way to make full use of every bit of suffering (big and small) that comes to us!

Did you get that?

God will show us how to *use* tragedy.

And we will either be open-minded and courageous enough to listen to Him and follow through, or we will let our grief swamp us and fill us with bitterness and throw us into a kind of despair that can ruin our lives!

Life's tragedies and hardships and heartbreaks, whether they come from death or illness or accident or broken friendships, can either make us or break us! All around us we see people who have been broken by their sorrow.

But just as surely, the hard knocks can *make* us! They can push us forward, if we let them!

If we are willing to follow the example of the Lord we claim to follow.

And this point will answer this question: "How does God comfort a Christian in time of sorrow and trouble? What does He do? The trouble is still there, isn't it?" Yes, the trouble may still be there. If your Mother is dead, you cannot bring her back. *But,* God comforts us by giving us a way to make actual creative *use* of the very thing that makes us cry!

". . . God of all comfort, who consoles us in our every trouble, so that we may be able to encourage those in any kind of distress, with the consolation with which we are divinely sustained" (II Cor. 1:4).

As Jesus Christ hung there on His Cross, He made *use* of His Suffering to save us! To show us that His Heart was a Heart of Love and that He couldn't possibly have cared more for us! He *used* His Suffering to *save* us! Now, He says to you and to me that we are to follow Him in *all* that He did!

And right now I know you are about to shout: "Yes, but He was God as He hung there on the Cross! I'm not God! I can't take suffering the way He did!"

But, wait a minute! Don't we as Christians believe the Holy Spirit and God are one and the same? Yes, we do. And if that is true, isn't God *in us* too? Jesus Christ never asks us to do anything He has not done under very similar circumstances. So, when He tells us we can *use* our suffering to comfort another, or perhaps to show them that Christians have a safe landing place even in the midst of trouble, I believe we can do it!

I know we can. I've tried it. And I mean to keep on trying it.

If you are in sorrow as you read this, please don't think I'm trying to belittle your grief or tell you it isn't important. It is important. It is so important to the Lord Jesus that He is sharing it with you right now! And He is saying to you, *"You and I* can take this thing and shine it up and find a way to use it so that you, My child, will grow in spiritual maturity and depth of character. Then, you will be able to help other people whose lives are also struck with sorrow."

Jesus is asking us all if we are *willing* to keep the poison of self-pity *out* of our wounds. Are we willing to follow Him and trust Him to heal us even when everything seems black and there seems to be no way out of our trouble?

Are there young people who have this kind of courageous, willing heart? Yes, and here is a part of a letter I received from a fifteen-year-old girl named Sue Ellen, who lives in Springfield, Illinois:

Dear Genie,
I am in the hospital as I write this, with a serious infection. I haven't been able to sleep nights for almost a week, I am so nervous and in so much pain. I guess I'll have to stay here quite a while. But, isn't the Lord wonderful to make it possible for me to be here at this nice hospital? What the doctors do hurts, but I am thankful for the care I'm getting. The Lord Jesus has done so much for me, I just can't find words to thank Him! Mother has gotten a lot worse. They have her under oxygen all the time now. She is on the next floor in the

hospital here, and I guess they are going to have to do heart surgery as a last resort to try to save her life. My Dad is as bad off as ever. He does not seem to want to take care of any of us six children. I'm the oldest, so if anything happens to Mother I'll have to look after them, I guess. I'm surely glad I'm a Christian, because I could never do it without the Lord Jesus living right in me and doing it through me, as you explained. The State is checking on my Dad now. Our home is broken up, but I know the Lord Jesus knows that it is and I intend to go through whatever hardships come just as I know He would want me to do! I surely do love Him, and it *is*, just as you said when I heard you speak that time, really exciting to be a Christian!

If you read this portion of Sue Ellen's letter hurriedly, I suggest that you read it again. *Nothing* was right in her life when she wrote that letter, and yet she was *using* it all by showing that radiant spirit in the midst of her trouble! We may not even be aware of how much we are using our sorrows to glorify God, or to help others. Sue Ellen had no idea that her letter to me would ever appear in a book! But, it's helped you, hasn't it? And it certainly helped me.

Sue Ellen didn't *need* to know the effect of her life at that moment. She just *needed to be in union* with Jesus and *willing to forget self-pity* and let Him show her how to *use* her trouble! By the time you read this, that letter will be over a year old. But, it will go on being used wherever this book is read. How does God comfort us? By His Presence, yes. But also by giving us a way not to *waste* our tears! You see, with Jesus Christ, even tears can be used to make something beautiful!

Isn't that what you'd really expect from a God who makes morning-glories grow out of little hard, ugly brown seeds?

13

How Can I Become a Christian?

"How can I become a Christian?"

In order to understand something about God's part in our becoming Christians, we need to have some knowledge of why He had to hang on that Cross and just what it was that happened when He did hang there almost two thousand years ago. We have already talked about this in another chapter, but for our purposes now, let's look at it this way: If we read our Bible we'll soon find out that Jesus Christ, when He was on earth, was calling all people *not* to a different way of thinking so much as to a different way of *living!* Jesus says we must return *good* for evil! Jesus Christ did not (as do so many cver-zealous Christians) go about telling people what dreadful sinners they were. He went about asking them point-blank to *follow Him!* And if we attempt to follow Jesus Christ even a little way, we find out *for ourselves,* in short order that we *are* sinners and that we would get nowhere following someone like Jesus, unless we were changed on the *inside!*

But even though God sees that we can't follow Him without this inner change, and even though He wants so much for us to follow Him, He *does not force us.* Your teacher or your parent may try to force you, but God will not. God will keep on wooing you in different ways through books and friends and directly through the prompting of His Spirit, because He loves you and needs you. But He will *not* force you!

Sometimes it seems almost too amazing to believe, but God *did* come to this earth in the form of a Man, Jesus Christ. This is the way He showed us what His Heart and Mind were like, as He went about showing people how to live this new, exciting life called Eternal Life. But *He did much more than teach!*

God, in Christ, let us see *inside* His Great Heart when headstrong, sinful man nailed Him to a Cross! And it is when we are allowed to look at this Heart that we are melted. If God is like this—I want to follow Him! If God is like Jesus Christ, then I *can* trust Him!

The Bible tells us that God was *in* Christ on that Cross, bridging the big gap between God and us. You know a bridge has to be built from both sides. Jesus Christ knew what it was like to be *us,* because He was human. But He also knew what it is like to be *God,* because He was Divine! So, *only* Jesus Christ could make that bridge between God and man, *from both sides at once.*

That's what He did on the Cross.

And when we make up our minds to put our *trust* in Jesus and to begin to follow Him, living our daily lives as He wants us to live them, *we are reconciled with God.* Our guilty feelings are gone. We are forgiven. Our slates are wiped clean. No matter what we've done, when Jesus Christ presents us to the Father as His followers, you and I are welcome!

And we are given a *new nature.*

Now, just what does it mean to be given a new nature? What does this new life mean? Does it mean that in an instant you are going to become like Christ? No. Because this is a LIFE we receive, and in *any* life there is growth! A baby can't get out of its cradle and ride a bicycle just because it has been born! It has to grow and develop muscles and a sense of balance and judgment. Then it can ride a bicycle—with practice!

So, we see that this new life *is*, just what Jesus said it is in the third chapter of the Gospel of John, being born all over again. And one of the best ways I have ever found of explaining this process (although it is not at all the whole explanation, since no one knows that but God) is to take a look at five different kingdoms. Four of these are already familiar to you if you've had a General Science course: (1) the *inorganic* kingdom, where there is *no life,* in which we find minerals, metals, etc.; (2) the *plant* kingdom, next above it, in which we find simple life; (3) the *animal* kingdom in which we find all animals except man; and (4) the kingdom of *man*, in which we find ourselves. But there is one more Kingdom if our list is to be complete, and that is the highest of all, the Kingdom of God.

We could make a "table" which would look something like this:

(1) Inorganic kingdom . . . sand, rocks, minerals (lifeless matter)

(2) Plant kingdom . . . . . grass, trees, flowers, etc. (growing things)

(3) Animal kingdom . . . . sheep, dogs, horses, etc. (animal life)

(4) Kingdom of man . . . . human beings (human life)

(5) Kingdom of God . . . Spiritual beings (Spiritual Life)

Now, each kingdom, from the lowest (inorganic) to the highest (spiritual) is sealed off from above. In other words, a grain of sand, no matter how much it "longed" (if a grain of sand *could* "long"!) could not lift itself *up* into the kingdom above it! The *inorganic kingdom*, the home of our "grain of sand," has no life in it. It is made up of lifeless matter. Crystals in salt, for example, are in this lifeless kingdom. They do not *grow*, they are *added to* by a process known as crystallization. And so the grain of sand is "stuck" where it is—in the lifeless realm, *until* the root of a clump of grass from the kingdom just above reaches *down* and lifts the grain of sand *up* into the *plant kingdom!* Then (but only then) can the grain of sand know *life*. It becomes a part of something infinitely greater than itself. It becomes a part of life itself. The lowly grain of sand is now a living part of a fine blade of green grass growing, we'll say, in a wide, sunny meadow. *But* before long, the blade of grass begins to yearn (if a blade of grass could yearn!) to be something higher! It "sees" the little wooly lambs gamboling about across the meadow, and the blade of grass longs to be a part of a kind of life in which there is *motion!* No amount of "longing," however, brings this about for the poor little blade of grass. It just *cannot* move itself *up* into the next kingdom above. So, not until the lamb chances to eat its way toward our ambitious blade of grass, can the "miracle" of changing kingdoms take place! But it does take place, when the lamb eats the grass, and once more there is a "lifting" into a higher kingdom. By the same procedure, though, the lamb stays in the *animal kingdom, until* you or I come along, hungry for a lamb chop! That's right—*up* goes the lamb into a still higher kingdom, the *kingdom of man.*

This is the kingdom into which you and I are born, "made in the image of God." But man has a big, empty space in the center of his being which sets up a longing so deep, no other member of any lower kingdom could understand it. Many members of our kingdom of man don't recognize what it is they want. They think it is fame, success, money, education, home, family, romance, fun, travel, music, art in many forms . . . oh, they call it by many, many names. Some even try to fill up that emptiness with alcohol and narcotics. But as soon as we reach the age when we know right from wrong, we all begin to feel this deep, restless longing.

We stand by a window looking out at the sunset and hear in the music we have playing on the phonograph, an echo of our own longing turning back upon us. We ache inside with a sadness we almost enjoy! Sometimes we are honest and courageous enough to admit we don't know what makes us ache so. But usually we say it's because we long to be with one certain person whom we can't have, or because we long to go to a certain party we weren't allowed to attend, or because we're not popular and sought after and so on and on and on. All of these things can be, and often are *symptoms* of the real reason we are longing down deep inside ourselves. But, in reality, I believe we are in the same predicament with the grain of sand and the blade of grass and the little lamb!

We are longing for something beyond ourselves. We are longing for *Someone* beyond ourselves. We are longing to be something higher and deeper than we are. We are longing for a kind of Love we have never found in the kingdom of man. We are longing for God. We are longing to be lifted up into a higher kingdom!

Now, you may not believe this as you read it. You may be saying, "That's not what *I* want! What I want is far from that!" I said that too for years and years. We may really believe that until we *try* God! But once we're lifted up into the next and highest kingdom, we know once and for all that *this* is what we've really been wanting! We called it by many other names. But it was this all along! A man named Augustine who lived a long, long time ago and who lived a very unChristian life for many years (as I did) said, after he had become a Christian: "Our hearts are restless until they rest in Thee!"

Old Augustine knew. So do I.

So do you if you've really been *lifted up* into the Realm of God.

But, you do not know if you've simply been going to church or to young people's meetings. Knowing Christians does not lift us up out of our ruts. It is knowing *Jesus Christ* that does it. And nothing else. A human mother can give birth to your body, but only God can give you a new spirit. And this is done when and only when the Spirit of God Himself (the Holy Spirit) comes to *invade* you — reaching down into the kingdom of man (where you are) from the Kingdom of God and lifting you up to *where God is.*

You won't be soaring bodily through space, but there will be times when your spirit will be so aware that it is actually in the Presence of God that it is the same as being lifted up. In reality, because space means nothing to God, the way in which He "lifts us up" *is to come into us Himself!*

So, when you open your life and receive Jesus Christ, you are receiving the very Life of God Himself in the Person of the Holy Spirit. The Holy Spirit is simply the means which God has arranged so that He can be with each one of us who will receive Him—every minute of every hour! When Jesus was on earth, He could only be with a few hundred people at a time. But now that

How Can I Become a Christian?

Jesus has gone in His Glorified Body to be with the Father, the Holy Spirit is *released* to come and live within us *all at once*, the only condition being that we receive Him and then give Him full possession of us!

Your question asked how *you* can become a Christian. There are many hundreds of ways and really only one. There are many procedures and methods. But God looks for the attitude of your heart! Only He knows whether or not you are really sincerely inviting Him to come in. And when Jesus was on earth, He Himself laid down the simplest and clearest method of procedure, I believe, when He said what is written down in the Gospel according to Luke, chapter 9, verse 23: "If anyone chooses to be my disciple, he must say 'No' to self, put the cross on his shoulders daily, and continue to follow me."* All of the things which Jesus told us to do are usually impossible for us. *But* they are not impossible for God, and remember—please remember—that when you receive Jesus Christ as your Personal Saviour, you literally receive the Life of God Himself into your life, so that then you are able to do what Jesus says and have a good time doing it! By "good time" I don't mean you are going to be shouting with laughter every minute. But down inside you that longing will be filled and you will have peace and the absolute knowledge that you are never alone!

In this verse (Luke 9:23) Jesus outlines four simple steps for receiving this new Life: (1) *"If anyone chooses to be my disciple."* You must make up your mind. This is your part—to decide first. (2)". . . *he must say 'No'*

* Translated by Charles B. Williams.

to self." This means you must be willing to obey Jesus instead of yourself at the points where you would disagree. In other words, you agree to agree with God right down the line, trusting Him to show you your mistakes and to change your desires so that you will find it easier and easier to agree with Him as time goes by. (3) ". . . *put the cross* on his shoulders." This is not the Cross of Christ. He has already borne that. This is our cross which is really our *responsibilities* as Christians. Be willing to "shoulder" your responsibilities to others. Allow Him *to give you* a sense of caring about other people as you may now care about yourself. (4) ". . . *and continue to follow me.*" The *continue* is important. True conversion to Jesus·Christ means a *daily surrendering* to Him in love and friendship. We *begin* at one certain time to follow Him, but unless we *continue,* we will find our friendship fading away. Any romance needs to be kindled and developed. *This* relationship with God is Romance with a capital R!

Jesus Christ is waiting at this moment to enter into this tremendous, Eternal Pact with *you!* The way has been cleared by what He did on the Cross, and the instant you put your faith in the One who hung on that Cross, your sins are forgiven, wiped out, *forgotten* by God the Father, who will open His Arms as He runs to meet you—because you have begun to agree with His Beloved Son, Jesus!

When you and I agree with Jesus Christ, we are clear with God and not only headed for heaven, but are lifted up into the highest Kingdom *now*—made members of the Family of God, because the Life of God is *put into* us right here on this old earth!

Naturally, this is too much for us to *understand.* But our understanding is not what God seeks. He wants *us!*

I'm glad this is what He wants. I like to be wanted just for myself, don't you? So does God. The real disciple receives Christ for Himself. Not merely for what He can give! If you will open your life to receive the Life of God right now, the same Power that brought the dead Body of Jesus up out of that grave, will be poured into *you!* This is an absolutely free gift from God to you because He loves you so much!

It seems backwards, doesn't it, that God should have to plead with us to take such a Gift?

14

How Can I Be Sure I'm a Christian?

"I think I've been converted, but how can I be sure I'm a Christian?"

"I told Jesus Christ I received Him as my Personal Saviour, but how can I know the new birth really happened to me?"

We said in the chapter before this one that we can't understand the new birth of Life within us. Neither can we explain it. It is a miracle of God, and there is nothing miraculous about the things *we* can explain! We can boss or command what we are able to explain. In the victorious life with Christ, the whole, big, glowing, wonderful secret is that we can relax and let Him tell *us* what to do! And then when we do it, our power is the Power of God. Of course, God will never force us to obey Him. Remember, He is Jesus Christ, and Jesus stands there

in all His Glory and Power and Strength and *asks* us to
follow Him for love's sake! Either we love Him enough
or we don't. Either we obey Him or we don't.

But when we do obey, the new life grows within
us and the very Spirit of God, Who lives within us *if* we
are Christians, begins to let *our* human spirits know that
we have truly been made Sons of God!

You know that when a witness is called upon to
testify in court, that witness knows something which can
add to the case, because he either saw or heard or ex-
perienced the thing in question. This is what Paul means
when he says in his letter to the Romans (chapter 8, verse
16): "This Spirit bears witness jointly with our spirits
that we are God's children."

The Spirit of God within you experiences your presence with Him, and your spirit experiences God's Presence
with you! This is the basis of real closeness. We are joint-
heirs with Christ to all God has for us as *real* Sons of God!
If you have received Jesus Christ as your Personal Saviour
and meant it in your heart, you have God's Own Word for
it that you are really a Son of God, born again into a
sonship equal with Christ! Seems almost too wonderful,
doesn't it? But in the Gospel of John the twelfth verse of
the first chapter gives us "God's Word" that this is true—
". . . to those who did accept Him [Jesus], He granted
ability to become God's children, that is, to those who
believe in His name."

If we can't believe God when He says something
to us, whom can we believe?

So then, the Spirit witnesses to our spirit and we

know by an inner certainty. *But,* if we are such new Christians that we haven't become sensitive enough to God's Spirit yet to catch this witness within us, we can simply plant our eternal lives right down on the FACT of God's Own Say-so in the Gospel of John!

". . . TO THOSE WHO ACCEPT HIM, HE GRANTED ABILITY [POWER] TO BECOME GOD'S CHILDREN [SONS OF GOD], THAT IS, TO THOSE WHO BELIEVE IN HIS NAME."

Human beings double-cross each other. Sometimes they lie. Sometimes they say something which they believe to be true, but which turns out not to be true because they were ignorant of the subject. This can never be so with God. God knows *everything* and He *cannot* lie. We can believe Him absolutely. And He says that when we have received Jesus Christ we are *given* the Power to become new creatures! We are given new Life. Christ Himself says in Revelation 3:20: "Here I stand knocking at the door. If anyone listens to My voice and opens the door, I will come in to him and dine with him and he with Me." Does Christ mean that? Unless He is wrong or misrepresenting things, He will come right in the minute we open the door to our lives and invite Him in.

And when He comes in, His Life comes in with Him and we have been born again into the Kingdom of God! None of this depends upon our *feeling.* Feelings are based on emotions. I want you to remember this and you will be far ahead of most adults in your Christian lives. Too many people expect God's Presence always to be accompanied by high spirits and deep joy or some kind of spiritual thrill. This is not always true. If it were true, being selfish by nature, we would be seeking God for the joy and thrills He could give, rather than for love of Him. So, keep these three points in your mind in this order:

First in importance is the FACT of Jesus Christ and what He did on the Cross for us.

Second in importance is our FAITH in this FACT of Jesus Christ and what He did for us.

Third in importance (behind both the other two) comes our FEELING. *It is not dependable at all.* Whether you feel God's Presence or not, God is always right there inside you because He Himself said, "I will neither give you up nor ever at all desert you . . . And, mind you, I am alongside you all the days until the end of the age." Just because you feel "in the dumps" or discouraged or disgusted does not mean for one instant that Jesus has left you! He said He would be with us forever, and He means every word He says!

We have already said that we know we can trust a God whose Character is like Jesus Christ. And so one of the most definite ways in which I *know* I have Eternal Life is through the Character of Jesus Christ Himself! I am sure of my salvation because I am sure of my Saviour! Even if people should stop believing in the "process" which we call salvation, it would not change the Saviour in any way! He is still the same and will be the same forever. "Jesus Christ [is] the same yesterday, today, and forever" (Hebrews 13:8). We may change but He does not. And in Jesus Christ, the very Word or Thought or Essence of God "became human and lived a little while among us." So the Object of my love, Jesus Christ Himself, is my guarantee of my salvation, *and* my standing with the Father.

There is still another way we can know whether or not we have been truly made new by God's Holy Spirit when we received Him. Jesus asks us to follow Him. "Follow Me" He asks over and over and over; and if you are finding it easier to follow Him and obey Him—even on *some* points—you may know for sure that you *are* born again.

But even more than this, we find another accurate test of our new lives in John's First Letter, chapter 3, verse 9: "No one who is born of God *makes a practice of sinning*, because the God-given life-principle continues to live in him, and so he cannot *practice* sinning, because he is born of God." *

The Christian forsakes sin. *If* the new Life of God has really been put within you, then you *cannot go on making a habit or practice of sinning!* Of course, we still have our free will and we can always choose whether we obey God or disobey Him. But just as we cannot knowingly hurt, and keep on hurting some human being we love, so we cannot knowingly hurt, and keep on hurting Jesus Christ, if we really love Him, and are really His followers. *Sin is so obvious in His Presence.* We all know that if we could *see* Him looking at us we would not disobey.

Many people get discouraged on this point. But remember, God is really within us if we have been truly

* Translated by Charles B. Williams.

made new by His Holy Spirit. God overpowered Satan on the Cross, and this Power within us comes to grips with our wills. And when in His strength we choose to follow Christ, this inner Power overpowers the sin!

Another accurate way to check on whether or not you have really been born again—with the Life of God actually put within you—is to check your personality against these signs that God's Spirit is living within you! If you have changed places with God and have really allowed Him to take over the living of your life day by day, then the people who live and play and work with you *will find you easier to live and play and work with!* Your disposition will be better. You won't fly off the handle the way you did once. You won't be so critical. You won't be unkind. You won't show partiality. You won't deliberately hurt people. You won't snub anyone. You won't try to shock people. You won't complain. You'll begin to lose your selfish habits.

According to Paul, in his letter to the Galatians, *these* are the products of the Spirit—or the signs in *your* disposition that show whether or not you are a true disciple of Jesus Christ: (Check yourself right now!)

(1) LOVE (Do you love people?)

(2) JOY (Do you love life?)

(3) PEACE (Are you peaceful or guilty? Are you a peacemaker or a trouble maker?)

(4) PATIENCE (Are you irritable? Do you love enough to be pleasant even when you are inconvenienced?)

(5) KINDNESS (Are you kind, even to strangers? To
members of other races? To grumpy people?
To everyone?)

(6) GOODNESS (Do you love goodness? Or do you
love evil? Remember e-v-i-l is l-i-v-e spelled
backwards!)

(7) FAITHFULNESS (Are you dependable? Do you
carry your load?)

(8) GENTLENESS (Are you a gentleman? Are you a
gentle-woman? Are you courteous?)

(9) SELF-CONTROL (Can you control yourself? Your
temper? Are you a glutton?)

These products of the Indwelling Holy Spirit sound
like a course in "how to become popular" or "how to be
a success," don't they? The end result is the same, except
that, with the Christian, God Himself does the hard part!
No human being, on his or her own will power can show
forth *all* these attractive personality traits . . . under *all*
circumstances. We might be able to produce some or all
of these traits some of the time, but in time of stress and
strain on the old nervous system, when we have dealings
with a certain kind of individual who "gets in our hair,"
we'll "blow our tops"—*if* we are doing it from within our
own selves.

But, if God is living His Life within us, we can
be sure that no one ever gets on the nerves of Jesus Christ!
And if Jesus Christ is our *Master* as well as our Saviour,
we show the definite signs of His Presence. You know,
people who are not Christian and don't pretend to be, are
pretty critical of those of us who call ourselves Christians.

How Can I Be Sure I'm a Christian?

They expect us to turn the other cheek because Jesus told us to do it. And they're right. There's nothing that gives us the desire really to *act* Christian as much as the realization that *we have the reputation of Jesus Christ in our hands wherever we go!* When we fall on our faces, He gets the blame! So, if we are real Christians, we will *act* like it! When we have faith in something or someone, we *act* like it! And one of the first, sure signs of the new life in Christ after conversion is that we begin to *act* differently. The real Spirit of Jesus Christ always shows up in us as the Spirit of Jesus Christ! Never any other spirit. If you are not more cooperative and considerate and kinder at home than you were before you became a Christian, how do you expect those who are not Christians to want what you have? Being a Christian is not being able to *say* that we believe certain things, but being willing to *act* like it! You can repeat until you are "blue in the face" that Jesus Christ died on the Cross to take away your sin, but if you go on being selfish and bad-tempered and critical and proud, no one is going to believe your sin has been taken away! Our actions as Christians speak far more clearly than all our words!

I have written this book especially for you if you are a young person. In this book are a lot of words. But if you should get to know me personally and find out that *I do not live up to what I have said to you, then you would have every right to throw the book back at me and tell me to forget the whole thing!*

I know a young woman named Janet whose weary mother asked her to help with the dishes after dinner one night. Janet grabbed her coat and flew out the door calling back in an irritated voice: "My goodness, Mother, can't you see I'm late already for our young people's committee meeting? We're starting a prayer group and I'm chairman! I can't take time to do dishes!"

Janet's brother, who was an alcoholic and not a Christian, stood in the kitchen doorway with a drink in his hand and laughed: "What's the matter with that brat? Doesn't she know we'd be more impressed if her religion began at home?" Janet's brother, who needed Christ so much, wanted no part of the brand of religion that showed up in unkindness even to those who loved her! If *this* selfish behavior showed the Spirit of the Christ which Janet kept telling her brother would "save" him from the bottle, then her brother wanted none of it. Do you see that Jesus took the blame?

We can depend on God Himself, and we can depend on His Promises in the Bible. We can absolutely put our weight down on the fact that if God went as far as He went on Calvary for us, surely He will go the rest of the way and come *in* to live within us when we invite Him.

But one of the best ways to be sure we are Christians is to watch our actions and our *reactions* in the times when the "going is tough." Before you were a Christian you would have done it one way. How would you do it now? Before you were a Christian you would have said one thing. What would you say now under the same conditions? Before you were a Christian, you could lie and forget it, providing you got by with it. How about now?

How Can I Be Sure I'm a Christian?

Before you were a Christian you were bored and always on the lookout for ways to fill up those "dull moments." How about now? In the light of who He *is* and what He *did* and what IIe offers you, aren't you about ready to agree with me that *only the real follower of this Tall, Strong, Living Lord Jesus can dare say that in his or in her life there is* NEVER A DULL MOMENT?

Or, if you haven't made the big decision and haven't entered into the Eternal Agreement yet, aren't you about ready to find out for yourself what it is that we Christians are excited about? It may still look "dull" to you from where you stand now, because it's only *after* you have allowed God to put HIS LIFE *in you,* that you can really get hold of what we mean when we say that the same Power that brought Jesus up out of that grave guarantees you NEVER A DULL MOMENT for all eternity!

CPSIA information can be obtained
at www.ICGtesting.com
Printed in the USA
JSRBC010741260221
12032JS00016B/40